Me and My Shadow

Wendy Blaxland

Illustrated by Teresa Culkin-Lawrence

Billy wanted his shadow to go away.

But his shadow seemed to say,
"Ha ha ha! Ho ho ho!
I will follow wherever you go.
I am your shadow, ho ho ho!"

Billy tried running through a door very fast and quickly closing the door behind him.

But when he turned around, there was his shadow.

It seemed to say,

"Ha ha ha! Hee hee hee!

Wherever you go, there I will be.

I am your shadow, hee hee hee!"

Billy tried staying in his bath for a long time
so his shadow would get soggy
and slip down the drain.

But when he got out of the bath
and wrapped himself in a towel,
his shadow was still there. It seemed to say,
"Hey hey hey! Hey hey hey!
I will never go away.
I am your shadow, hey hey hey!"

Billy tried cutting his shadow off.

He tried stomping on it.

He even tried turning off the light.
But when he switched the light back on,
his shadow was still there.

Billy sat on his bed in a grumpy mood
and clenched his fists.
The shadow of his hands looked like two animal faces,
and his shadow seemed to say,
"Ha ha ha! Ho ho ho!
I can be fun! I can put on a show!"

Billy wiggled his thumbs.

The shadow of his hands turned into dogs.

Then there were rabbits and giraffes and elephants.

Billy and his shadow made a shadow zoo.

"Ha ha ha! Hee hee hee," yawned his shadow.
"Let's go to sleep now, you and me."
So Billy snuggled down into bed with his shadow,
and they dreamed of what they could do together
in the morning.

McCall's
Fish and Fowl
COOKBOOK

BY THE FOOD EDITORS OF McCALL'S

Designed by Margot L. Wolf

PUBLISHED BY ADVANCE PUBLISHERS   P.O. BOX 7200, ORLANDO,FL 32854

Contents

Acknowledgments: All photographs are by George Ratkai.

Fish and Shellfish

FRESH OR FROZEN FISH

Fresh fish is good all the days of the year when you want a change from meat. McCall's suggests you try our recipes – if you like fish-with-a-difference. Fish provide a variety of nutritive factors. Rich in protein, in minerals and vitamins, they are a valuable addition to the diet, especially of the calorie-conscious.

Purchasing Hints

In selecting fresh fish, observe these points:

Eyes: Should be clean, clear, bright, full, and bulging. Redness is not an indication of spoilage – the eyes may have been bruised when fish was caught or in packing.

Gills: Reddish-pink, free from odor, slime, and discoloration.

Scales: Should have a characteristic sheen, adhere tightly to the skin, without slime.

Flesh: Should be firm and elastic, and spring back under pressure of your finger. The flesh should not be separated from the bones.

Odor: Fish when it's fresh has a clean, fresh odor, free from objectionable and stale smells.

Amounts to buy: A third to a half-pound of fresh fish per serving. If you serve a whole small fish, choose one weighing a pound for one serving.

Storage

Fresh fish should be wrapped in moisture-proof, air-tight material, or placed in a container and stored in the refrigerator immediately. If you intend to keep it for several days, freeze it in moisture-vapor-proof freezer paper or container. Properly wrapped and frozen, it will not spoil as long as it remains solidly frozen. Once it has thawed do not refreeze. It should remain packaged and refrigerated while thawing. If you want to thaw it quickly, place it under cold running water.

MARKET FORMS OF FISH

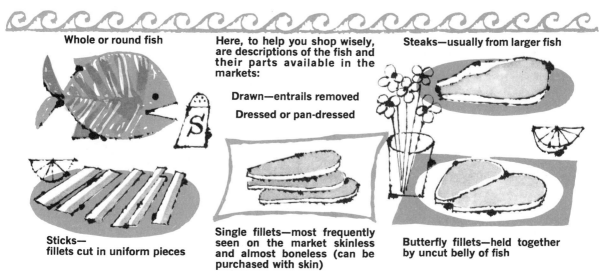

Whole or round fish

Here, to help you shop wisely, are descriptions of the fish and their parts available in the markets:

Drawn—entrails removed

Dressed or pan-dressed

Steaks—usually from larger fish

Sticks— fillets cut in uniform pieces

Single fillets—most frequently seen on the market skinless and almost boneless (can be purchased with skin)

Butterfly fillets—held together by uncut belly of fish

BROILED FISH

1. Let frozen fish thaw completely before broiling. Wash fish in cold water; pat dry with paper towels.
2. Lightly brush broiler rack with salad oil; arrange fish on rack. Brush fish with one of basting sauces, below.
3. Broil, 4 inches from heat as directed in timetable, below, or until fish flakes easily when tested with fork but is still moist.
4. To serve: Remove fish to heated platter. Garnish with lemon wedges and parsley sprigs. Pass one of sauces for fish, pages 27-28, if desired.

HERBED BASTING SAUCE: Combine 2 tablespoons salad oil, 2 tablespoons lemon juice, 1/4 teaspoon paprika, and 1/4 teaspoon dried marjoram, basil, or thyme leaves. Use to brush on fish several times during broiling.

CURRIED BASTING SAUCE: Combine 2 tablespoons salad oil, 2 tablespoons lemon juice, and 1/4 teaspoon curry powder. Use to brush on fish several times during broiling.

LEMONY BASTING SAUCE: Combine 3 tablespoons lemon juice with 1/8 teaspoon dry mustard, and 1 bay leaf, crumbled. Use to brush on fish several times during broiling.

TIMETABLE FOR BROILING FISH

Fish	Approximate time on each side
Fillets	5 to 8 minutes
Steaks	5 to 8 minutes
Dressed whole	5 minutes per pound
Split	5 to 8 minutes

BROILED SWORDFISH WITH BARBECUE SAUCE

3 lb swordfish steaks, 3/4 inch thick	1/4 cup finely chopped green pepper
2 teaspoons salt	1/2 cup chili sauce
1/2 teaspoon pepper	1/2 cup catsup
1/2 teaspoon seasoned salt	1/3 cup lemon juice
5 tablespoons butter or margarine	2 tablespoons light-brown sugar
1/4 cup finely chopped onion	1 teaspoon dry mustard
	1 tablespoon Worcestershire sauce
	1/2 cup water

1. Wipe steaks with damp cloth.
2. Combine 1 teaspoon salt, 1/4 teaspoon pepper, and the seasoned salt; use to sprinkle both sides of fish.
3. Arrange on greased rack in broiler pan. Dot lightly with 1 tablespoon butter; broil, 4 inches from heat, 5 minutes.
4. Turn fish; dot with 1 tablespoon butter, and broil 7 minutes longer.

5. Meanwhile, make barbecue sauce: In 3 tablespoons hot butter in medium skillet, sauté onion and green pepper until tender – about 5 minutes.
6. Add rest of ingredients, 1/2 cup water and remaining salt and pepper.
7. Simmer, uncovered, 10 minutes. Serve over swordfish.
MAKES 6 SERVINGS

CRISPY SALMON STEAKS

1/2 cup butter or margarine, melted	1 cup crushed potato chips
1 teaspoon salt	6 (6- to 8-oz size) salmon steaks, 3/4 inch thick
1/8 teaspoon paprika	6 lemon wedges
1 cup crushed saltines	6 parsley sprigs

1. Combine butter, salt and paprika. Combine saltines and potato chips.
2. Wipe steaks with damp cloth. Dip each into butter mixture; then roll in saltine mixture.
3. Arrange steaks on lightly greased broiler rack in broiler pan. Broil, 6 inches from heat, 5 to 8 minutes.
4. Turn; broil 5 to 8 minutes longer, or until fish flakes easily with fork. Serve each steak with a lemon wedge and parsley sprig.
MAKES 6 SERVINGS

BROILED SALMON OR SWORDFISH STEAKS WITH PARLSEY-LEMON BUTTER

4 salmon or swordfish steaks, 1/2 inch thick	**Parsley-Lemon Butter**
1/4 cup butter or margarine, melted	1/4 cup butter or margarine
1 1/2 teaspoons seasoned salt	2 tablespoons lemon juice
	2 tablespoons chopped parsley

1. Rinse salmon steaks under cold running water; drain; pat dry with paper towels.
2. Place salmon on rack of broiler pan. Brush with 2 tablespoons melted butter; sprinkle with 3/4 teaspoon seasoned salt.
3. Broil, 4 inches from heat, 10 minutes. Turn salmon; brush with remaining melted butter, and sprinkle with remaining seasoned salt. Broil 8 minutes longer, or until fish flakes easily when tested with a fork.
4. Meanwhile, make Parsley-Lemon Butter: Melt butter in small saucepan. Stir in lemon juice and parsley. Keep warm.
5. Remove salmon to heated serving platter. Pour lemon butter over salmon.
MAKES 4 SERVINGS

CHEESE-BAKED HALIBUT

2½ lb halibut steaks, ¾ inch thick
¼ cup lemon juice
¼ teaspoon salt
⅛ teaspoon pepper
¼ teaspoon dried thyme leaves

1 cup grated Swiss cheese (¼ lb)
¼ cup packaged dry bread crumbs
¼ cup butter or margarine, melted

1. Preheat oven to 375F. Lightly grease a large, shallow baking dish.
2. Wipe halibut with damp cloth; place halibut in dish. Pour lemon juice over fish. Then sprinkle with salt, pepper, and thyme.
3. Bake, uncovered, 20 minutes.
4. Meanwhile, combine cheese and bread crumbs. Sprinkle fish with cheese mixture, then melted butter.
5. Bake 10 minutes longer, or until fish flakes easily with fork. Serve right from baking dish.
MAKES 6 SERVINGS

STEAMED WHOLE FISH

3-lb whole fish, head and tail on, cleaned and scaled (red snapper, sea bass or baby striped bass)
1 bunch green onions, washed and thinly sliced on diagonal

½ lb fresh mushrooms, washed and thinly sliced lengthwise through stem
2 tablespoons chopped parsley
1 teaspoon salt
1 tablespoon soy sauce
1 tablespoon lemon juice

1. Wash fish under cold running water; dry with paper towels. Arrange on heatproof platter.
2. Sprinkle with onion, mushrooms, parsley and salt. Mix soy sauce and lemon juice; sprinkle over fish. Place platter on rack set over roasting pan half-filled with water and placed over burners. Cover, pan and all, with foil.
3. Steam over medium heat 40 to 45 minutes, or until fish flakes easily when tested with fork.
MAKES 6 SERVINGS

BAKED STUFFED FISH

1 whole red snapper, striped bass, cod, haddock, bluefish, or whitefish, cleaned (2½ to 3 lb)

Stuffing
¼ cup butter or margarine
½ cup chopped onion
½ cup chopped celery

2 tablespoons chopped parsley
½ teaspoon salt
½ teaspoon dried thyme leaves
1 cup fresh bread cubes (2 slices)

3 slices bacon
Pepper

1. Wash fish inside and out under cold running water. Drain well; pat dry with paper towels.
2. Make Stuffing: In hot butter in medium skillet, sauté onion and celery until tender – about 5 minutes. Add the chopped parsley, ½ teaspoon salt, the thyme, and bread cubes; toss to mix well.
3. Preheat oven to 400F.
4. Spoon stuffing into cavity; close opening with skewers or wooden picks.
5. Place fish in large, greased roasting pan. Arrange bacon, not overlapping, lengthwise over top of fish; sprinkle with pepper.
6. Bake 35 to 40 minutes, or until fish flakes easily when tested with a fork and bacon is crisp.
7. To serve: Remove fish to heated serving platter. Sprinkle with additional chopped parsley, if you wish.
MAKES 6 TO 8 SERVINGS

BAKED STRIPED BASS

4- to 5-lb whole striped bass with head, cleaned
2 teaspoons salt
1 small lemon
Parsley
1 cup thinly sliced onion
½ cup thinly sliced carrot
½ cup thinly sliced celery

½ teaspoon dried thyme leaves
1 bay leaf
1 cup dry white wine
½ cup water
¼ cup butter or margarine, melted

Lemon Butter, page 6

1. Preheat oven to 400F. Lightly grease a shallow roasting pan.
2. Wash fish inside and out under cold water; pat dry with paper towels. Sprinkle fish inside and out with the salt.
3. Slice lemon thinly; cut slices in quarters. With small, sharp-pointed knife, make deep cuts, about 2 inches apart, along both sides of fish. With fingers, press a piece of lemon and a small sprig of parsley into each cut.
4. Place fish in prepared pan. Add any remaining lemon slices and parsley, along with onion, carrot, celery, thyme, and bay leaf. Pour in wine and ½ cup water. Pour butter over fish.
5. Bake, basting frequently with liquid in pan, 30 to 40 minutes, or until fish flakes easily when tested with a fork.
6. With large spatulas, carefully lift fish to heated serving platter. With slotted spoon, lift out vegetables, and place around fish. Vegetables will be on the crisp side. Garnish platter with parsley and lemon, if desired. Serve with Lemon Butter.
MAKES 6 SERVINGS

LEMON BUTTER

6 tablespoons butter or margarine

2 tablespoons lemon juice

1. In a small skillet or saucepan, heat butter over medium heat until it foams and becomes light brown.
2. Remove from heat. Stir in lemon juice. Serve at once.
MAKES 6 SERVINGS

BAKED HADDOCK, NEW ENGLAND STYLE

1 fresh haddock (3½ lb), cleaned, head and tail removed

1½ teaspoons seasoned salt

Pepper

2 tablespoons lemon juice

Cracker Topping

½ cup crushed unsalted crackers

½ cup chopped, fresh mushrooms

¼ cup thinly sliced green onions

2 tablespoons chopped parsley

1½ teaspoons seasoned salt

⅛ teaspoon pepper

¼ cup butter or margarine, melted

2 tablespoons lemon juice

6 slices bacon

1. Wash fish in cold water; pat dry with paper towels. With sharp knife, carefully remove bones, keeping fish joined down back (or have fish boned at market).
2. Preheat oven to 400F. Line a 13-by-9-by-2-inch baking pan with foil; butter foil.
3. Sprinkle inside of boned fish with ¾ teaspoon seasoned salt, dash pepper and 1 tablespoon lemon juice. Fold fish lengthwise; place in pan. Sprinkle with ¾ teaspoon seasoned salt, dash pepper and 1 tablespoon lemon juice.
4. **Make Cracker Topping.** Combine crushed crackers, mushrooms, green onion, parsley, seasoned salt and pepper in medium bowl; mix. Add melted butter and lemon juice; toss until well combined.
5. Spoon over fish in a 3-inch wide layer. Arrange bacon diagonally on top.
6. Bake, basting every 10 minutes with pan juices, 30 to 35 minutes, or until fish flakes easily with a fork.
7. Carefully lift fish to heated serving platter. Garnish with parsley and lemon wedges, if desired.
MAKES 6 SERVINGS

TROUT AMANDINE

4 (½-lb size) rainbow trout, cleaned, with head and tail on

⅓ cup all-purpose flour

½ teaspoon salt

Dash pepper

¼ cup milk

Butter or margarine

⅓ cup sliced almonds

1. Wash fish under cold running water. Drain; pat dry with paper towels.
2. On 12-inch square of waxed paper, combine flour, salt, and pepper.
3. Pour milk into 9-inch pie plate. Dip trout in milk; shake off excess; roll in flour mixture until well coated.
4. In large skillet, over medium heat, heat ¼ cup butter until golden. Add trout; sauté, over medium heat, 5 minutes, or until underside is browned. Turn, being careful not to break fish; sauté 5 minutes, or until fish are browned and flake easily when tested with a fork.
5. Carefully remove fish to heated serving platter.
6. Add ¼ cup butter to skillet. When melted, add almonds; sauté over low heat until almonds are pale golden. Pour almonds and butter over fish. Serve immediately.
MAKES 6 SERVINGS
Note: If you use frozen trout, thaw them completely.

SEAFOOD AND VEGETABLES EN CASSEROLE

1 lb thawed frozen fillets (halibut, haddock or cod)

2 tablespoons butter or margarine

¼ cup chopped onion

¼ lb mushrooms, sliced

2 tablespoons all-purpose flour

½ cup milk

¼ teaspoon salt

Dash pepper

½ cup white wine

1 pkg (10 oz) frozen mixed vegetables

2 cups hot, seasoned, freshly mashed potato

2 tablespoons butter or margarine, melted

2 tablespoons grated Parmesan cheese

1. Cut fish into 2-inch pieces.
2. In 2 tablespoons hot butter in skillet, sauté chopped onion and sliced mushrooms, stirring, about 5 minutes. Remove from heat; stir in flour; then gradually stir in milk. Add salt and pepper.
3. Bring to boiling, stirring; boil until sauce thickens; reduce heat; stir in wine. Add fish and mixed vegetables; simmer, covered and stirring once or twice, 10 minutes, or until vegetables and fish are tender.
4. Turn into four individual baking shells or a 4-cup casserole. Spoon mashed potato around edge of each; or, put potato through pastry bag with a number-5 star tip, to form a decorative edge.
5. Drizzle melted butter over top. Sprinkle with grated Parmesan cheese. Run under broiler a few minutes, until nicely browned.
MAKES 4 SERVINGS

FILLETS OF SOLE DUGLÈRE

6 fillets of sole (about 2½ lb) (see Note)
3 tablespoon lemon juice
3 tablespoons butter or margarine
4 medium fresh mushrooms, sliced
1 teaspoon salt
Dash pepper
1 cup dry white wine
¼ cup water
4 medium tomatoes (1½ lb)

Sauce
¼ cup butter or margarine
¼ cup all-purpose flour
½ teaspoon salt
Dash ground black pepper
1½ cups fish stock
¾ cup grated Parmesan cheese
3 tablespoons dry bread crumbs
2 tablespoons butter or margarine, melted

1. Preheat oven to 350F. Lightly butter 13-by-9-by-2-inch baking dish.
2. Rinse fillets under cold water; pat dry with paper towels. Brush with 2 tablespoons lemon juice. Fold crosswise; place in prepared dish.
3. Melt 3 tablespoons butter in small saucepan. Add mushrooms; sprinkle with 1 tablespoon lemon juice, 1 teaspoon salt, and the pepper; toss. Add wine and ¼ cup water; bring to boiling. Pour over fish.
4. Lightly butter one side of a double thickness of waxed paper; place, buttered side down, over fish.
5. Bake 15 to 20 minutes, or just until fish flakes easily when tested with a fork.

6. Meanwhile, scald tomatoes, and peel. Cut in quarters; scrape seeds and center pulp into a sieve set over a bowl; press through sieve. (You should have ¾ cup purée.) Set aside. Dice outer part of tomato. Set aside.
7. Carefully remove fish from baking dish, and arrange, slightly overlapping, in shallow 1½- or 2-quart broilerproof serving dish. Top with the mushrooms. Cover; keep warm.
8. Strain fish stock into a 2-cup measure. Reserve 1½ cups for sauce.
9. **Make Sauce.** Melt ¼ cup butter in medium saucepan. Remove from heat; stir in flour, salt, and pepper. Stir in 1½ cups fish stock and the tomato purée; cook over medium heat, stirring constantly, until mixture thickens and comes to boiling.
10. Stir in ½ cup Parmesan. Return to boiling, stirring constantly; reduce heat; simmer 5 minutes. Add diced tomato.
11. Pour off liquid from fish and mushrooms. Spoon sauce over all.
12. In small bowl, toss bread crumbs and melted butter. Sprinkle over sauce; then sprinkle with remaining Parmesan.
13. Run dish under broiler 3 to 5 minutes, or until top is golden-brown.
MAKES 6 SERVINGS

Note: If using frozen sole, let thaw completely.

Seafood and Vegetables en Casserole

FILLET OF SOLE BEAULIEU

Rice Turban

1 can (10¾ oz) condensed chicken broth, undiluted
1¼ cups dry white wine
½ teaspoon dried tarragon leaves
¼ teaspoon dried basil leaves
1½ cups water
2 cups converted white rice
4 large fillets of sole (about 2½ lb)
2 tablespoons lemon juice
1 clove garlic, crushed
½ teaspoon dried tarragon leaves
½ teaspoon dried basil leaves

1 cup dry white wine

Sauce

3 tablespoons butter or margarine
1 teaspoon chopped shallot
1 teaspoon chopped parsley
1 tablespoon all-purpose flour
3 tablespoons tomato paste
½ teaspoon salt
Dash ground red pepper
⅔ cup heavy cream
¼ cup dry white wine
1 can (4½ oz) shrimp, or ½ lb fresh shrimp, cooked and cleaned

1. **Make Rice Turban.** In heavy, medium saucepan, combine broth, 1¼ cups wine, ½ teaspoon tarragon, ¼ teaspoon basil, and 1½ cups water; mix well.
2. Bring to boiling; add rice. Return to boiling; reduce heat, and cook, covered, 25 minutes, or until rice is tender and liquid is all absorbed. Turn into a lightly buttered 1½-quart Turk's-head or ring mold, about 8 inches in diameter. Place in low oven, about 300F, to keep warm.
3. While rice is cooking, wash fillets; dry well with paper towels. Brush both sides with lemon juice. Cut fillets in half lengthwise; roll up. Arrange in a single layer in skillet.
4. Sprinkle garlic, tarragon, and basil over fish. Add white wine; bring to boiling.
5. Reduce heat; simmer, covered, 10 to 15 minutes, or until fish flakes easily when tested with fork.
6. Remove fillets from cooking liquid; drain well. Strain liquid; measure 1 cup for sauce. Arrange fillets on hot serving platter (keep warm in oven while making sauce).

7. **Make Sauce.** In hot butter in medium saucepan, sauté shallot and parsley several minutes. Remove from heat; stir in flour, tomato paste, salt, and pepper; then gradually stir in 1 cup fish liquid and the cream. Bring to boiling, stirring, until thickened and smooth. Add wine and shrimp; heat several minutes.
8. Unmold rice in center of serving platter, with fillets surrounding it. Spoon sauce with shrimp over each fillet. Pass rest of sauce.
MAKES 6 SERVINGS

FILLETS OF SOLE FLORENTINE

Hollandaise Sauce, page 28

6 fillets of sole (2½ lb)
¼ cup lemon juice
2 tablespoons finely chopped shallot
2 teaspoons dried tarragon leaves
1 teaspoon salt
1 cup dry white wine
2 pkg (10-oz size) frozen chopped spinach

Wine Sauce

3 tablespoons butter or margarine
3 tablespoons all-purpose flour
½ teaspoon salt
⅛ teaspoon pepper
1 cup fish stock
⅓ cup light cream
½ cup heavy cream

1. **Make Hollandaise Sauce.** Let cool completely.
2. Rinse fillets under cool water; pat dry with paper towels. Brush both sides with lemon juice. Fold into thirds, with dark side inside. Arrange in single layer in large skillet. Sprinkle with shallot, tarragon and 1 teaspoon salt. Pour on wine.
3. Bring to boiling; reduce heat; simmer, covered, 5 to 10 minutes, or until fish flakes easily when tested with a fork. Do not overcook.
4. Meanwhile, cook the spinach as package label directs. Turn into a sieve; drain well, pressing spinach to remove all liquid. Return to saucepan; cover; keep hot.
5. With slotted spatula, remove fillets to heated platter; set aside; keep warm. Strain liquid from skillet into 2-cup measure. (You should have about 1 cup. Boil down if necessary.)

6. **Make Wine Sauce.** Melt butter in small saucepan. Remove from heat. Stir in flour, salt and pepper until smooth. Gradually stir in the fish stock and light cream.
7. Bring to boiling over medium heat, stirring constantly until mixture thickens. Remove from heat.
8. Stir ⅓ cup wine sauce into spinach; toss. Turn into a 12-by-8-by-2-inch broilerproof dish; spread evenly.
9. Arrange fillets in single layer on spinach. Spoon remaining wine sauce over fillets.
10. Beat heavy cream until stiff. Fold into hollandaise sauce. Spoon mixture over wine sauce.
11. Place under broiler 2 to 3 minutes, or until top is golden-brown.
MAKES 6 SERVINGS

Fillet of Sole Beaulieu ▶

FILLETS OF SOLE BONNE FEMME

4 tablespoons butter or margarine
2 shallots, chopped
6 sole, haddock, or flounder fillets (about 2½ lb)
½ lb fresh mushrooms, sliced
1 teaspoon salt
⅛ teaspoon pepper
1 cup white wine
1 tablespoon chopped parsley
1½ tablespoons all-purpose flour

1. Melt 2 tablespoons butter in large skillet. Add shallots, and sauté 2 minutes.
2. Wash fillets; dry on paper towels. Arrange fish over shallots, and top with mushrooms. Sprinkle salt and pepper over all. Add wine.
3. Bring to boiling; reduce heat, and simmer, covered, 10 minutes. Add parsley; cook 5 minutes longer, or until fish flakes easily with fork.
4. Drain fish well, reserving 1 cup liquid. Arrange fish and mushrooms in 12-by-8-by-2-inch baking dish.
5. Melt remaining butter in same skillet; remove from heat. Stir in flour until smooth. Gradually stir in reserved fish liquid.
6. Cook over medium heat, stirring, until thickened. Pour over fish. Run under broiler 3 to 5 minutes, or until top is golden-brown.
MAKES 6 SERVINGS

FILLETS OF SOLE QUEEN VICTORIA

8 fillets of sole (2½ lb)
1 egg white
¾ cup heavy cream
½ teaspoon salt
2 tablespoons chopped parsley
3 drops liquid hot-pepper seasoning
1 cup dry white wine
½ cup water
1 small onion, thinly sliced
3 slices lemon
1 bay leaf
3 whole black peppercorns
1 teaspoon salt
¼ teaspoon dried tarragon leaves
Newburg Sauce, below

1. Rinse fillets under cold water; pat dry with paper towels.
2. Select 6 best fillets; set aside. Cut 2 remaining fillets into 1-inch strips. Place strips in electric-blender container. Add egg white, cream, ½ teaspoon salt, the parsley, and hot-pepper seasoning. Blend, at high speed, 2 minutes, or until mixture is smooth and an even light-green color.
3. Place the 6 reserved fillets, skin side up, on a cutting board. Spoon fish mixture on each, dividing evenly (about 2 rounded tablespoonfuls each). Spread into an even layer, keeping it about half an inch from edges. Starting at narrow end, roll up fillets. Fasten with wooden picks.
4. Lightly butter a deep medium skillet or Dutch oven. Stand fillets on more even end, barely touching side of pan, to keep upright.

5. Add wine, ½ cup water, the onion, lemon, bay leaf, black peppercorns, salt, tarragon. Bring just to boiling; cover; reduce heat to low; simmer 10 to 15 minutes, or till fish mixture in center is firm when tested with fork.
6. Remove with slotted spatula; drain very well. (Reserve stock for sauce.) Place on heated serving platter. Top with some Newburg Sauce; pass remaining sauce.
MAKES 6 SERVINGS

NEWBURG SAUCE

3 tablespoons butter or margarine
2 tablespoons all-purpose flour
¼ teaspoon salt
⅛ teaspoon paprika
¾ cup light cream
½ cup fish stock*
2 egg yolks
2 tablespoons dry sherry
*Use liquid from cooking fish or bottled clam broth.

1. Melt butter in medium saucepan. Remove from heat; stir in flour, salt, and paprika until blended. Gradually stir in cream and fish stock.
2. Cook, over medium heat and stirring constantly, until mixture thickens and comes to boiling; boil 1 minute. Remove from heat.
3. In medium bowl, beat egg yolks well. Stir in about ½ cup hot sauce; then stir egg-yolk mixture into sauce in saucepan. Add sherry.
4. Cook over low heat, stirring, until heated through. Do not boil.
MAKES 1½ CUPS
*Reserved in step 6 above.

SEVICHE

1 lb fresh or thawed frozen fillets of flounder or sole
½ cup lime juice
1 teaspoon salt
2 medium onions, thinly sliced
2 medium oranges
2 medium tomatoes
¼ cup chopped scallion

1. Day before: Wash fillets; drain well. Arrange in one layer in a 12-by-8-by-2-inch glass dish.
2. Pour lime juice over fillets. Turn each one to coat well. Sprinkle with salt. Top with sliced onion.
3. Cover tightly with plastic wrap. Refrigerate 8 hours or overnight, turning fish fillets once more.
4. To serve: Wash, peel and slice oranges; reserve peel. Wash and slice tomatoes. Alternate sliced oranges and tomatoes around the edge of a serving platter. Make a row of onion slices, overlapping the bottoms of the orange and tomato slices.
5. Arrange fish fillets in center of platter. Sprinkle chopped scallion around fish fillets.
6. Remove white from back of some orange peel. Slice peel into ⅛-inch strips; arrange over fish fillets. Spoon lime-juice marinade over all.
MAKES 4 SERVINGS

BREADED COD FILLETS

2 lb cod fillets
1 egg
½ cup dry bread crumbs,
  or ½ cup packaged
  seasoned coating mix
  for fish
1 teaspoon salt

¼ teaspoon pepper
6 tablespoons butter or
  margarine

Parsley
Lemon wedges
Tartar Sauce, page 28

1. Rinse fillets in cold water; pat dry with paper towels. Cut in serving-size pieces.
2. In pie plate, beat egg with a fork until mixed. On waxed paper, mix crumbs, salt, pepper. (Omit salt and pepper if using coating mix.)
3. Dip fish in egg, to moisten both sides; then dip in crumbs, to coat well.
4. In large skillet, heat butter until it sizzles. Add fish pieces in a single layer. Sauté over medium heat until underside is golden-brown – about 5 minutes. Turn with spatula; sauté 5 minutes longer, to brown other side and until fish flakes easily when tested with a fork.
5. Remove to heated serving platter. Garnish with parsley and wedges of lemon. Serve with Tartar Sauce.
MAKES 6 SERVINGS

HADDOCK WITH HERB STUFFING

3 tablespoons butter or
  margarine
½ cup chopped onion
½ cup chopped celery
1 can (3 oz) chopped
  mushrooms, drained;
  or ½ cup chopped fresh
  mushrooms
2 cups day-old soft bread
  crumbs
1 teaspoon salt

⅛ teaspoon pepper
⅛ teaspoon dried
  tarragon leaves
⅛ teaspoon dried
  rosemary leaves
2 lb haddock fillets
3 tablespoons lemon
  juice
3 tomatoes, sliced ¼
  inch thick

1. Preheat oven to 375F. Lightly grease a large, shallow baking dish.
2. In hot butter in saucepan, sauté onion, celery, and mushrooms until onion is golden – about 5 minutes.
3. In large bowl, toss sautéed vegetables with bread crumbs, salt, pepper, tarragon, and rosemary until well mixed.
4. Wash fillets, and dry well on paper towels. Arrange in single layer in baking dish. Sprinkle with lemon juice. Spread herb stuffing over fish.
5. Then add layer of sliced tomatoes; bake, uncovered, 35 to 40 minutes, or until fish is easily flaked with fork. Serve right from baking dish.
MAKES 6 SERVINGS

FINNAN HADDIE DELMONICO

1½-lb piece smoked
  haddock
¼ cup butter or
  margarine
3 tablespoons all-
  purpose flour
½ teaspoon salt

Dash ground red pepper
1 cup milk
1 cup light cream

4 hard-cooked eggs
4 thin slices buttered
  toast

1. Rinse fish in cold water. If large, cut in half. Place in medium skillet. Add water to cover; bring to boiling; reduce heat; simmer, covered, 15 minutes.
2. Drain well. With a fork, separate fish into flakes. (You should have 2 cups.) Set aside.
3. Melt butter in medium saucepan. Remove from heat; blend in flour, salt, and pepper. Gradually stir in milk and cream.
4. Bring to boiling over medium heat, stirring. Reduce heat; simmer 5 minutes, stirring occasionally.
5. Peel eggs; slice 3, and chop 1. Cut toast into triangles.
6. Add fish and sliced egg to sauce; simmer 1 minute.
7. Turn into heated shallow serving dish. Sprinkle with chopped egg; arrange toast triangles around edge. Serve immediately.
MAKES 6 SERVINGS

NEW ENGLAND FISH CHOWDER

2 lb halibut fillets
8 slices bacon, cut in
  ½-inch pieces
1½ cups chopped onion
3 cups diced (¼-inch),
  pared potato
3 teaspoons salt

2 cups boiling water
3 cups milk
1 cup light cream
⅛ teaspoon pepper
Dash ground red pepper

Common crackers

1. Rinse fillets under cold water; drain. Cut in ½-inch pieces.
2. In 6-quart Dutch oven or kettle, sauté bacon until almost crisp. Pour off bacon fat; return 2 tablespoons fat to Dutch oven; discard the rest.
3. Add onion, and sauté until golden – about 5 minutes.
4. Add potato, 1 teaspoon salt, and the boiling water. Bring to boiling; reduce heat; simmer, covered, 10 minutes. Add fish; simmer, covered, 10 minutes longer.
5. Heat milk, cream to lukewarm.
6. Add milk mixture, remaining salt, and both of the peppers to chowder. Heat over low heat just until bubbles appear around edge of pan. Do not let boil.
7. Ladle into bowls. Float split common crackers on each serving.
MAKES 12 SERVINGS

Deep-Dish
Salmon
Potato Pie

CANNED OR PACKAGED FISH

DEEP-DISH SALMON (OR TUNA) POTATO PIE

½ pkg (11-oz size)
  piecrust mix

Sauce
¼ cup butter or
  margarine
⅓ cup all-purpose flour
2½ teaspoons salt
¼ teaspoon pepper
⅛ teaspoon paprika
2 cups milk
Boiling water
2 lb potatoes, peeled and
  thinly sliced

4 carrots, pared and
  thinly sliced
Butter or margarine
3 medium onions, thinly
  sliced
1 can (15 oz) salmon,
  drained, or 2 cans
  (6½-oz size) chunk light
  tuna, drained
1 egg yolk, mixed with 1
  tablespoon water

1. Prepare pastry as package label directs for a one-crust pie. Refrigerate until ready to use.
2. Preheat oven to 350F. Grease well a 2-quart oval casserole or baking dish.
3. **Make Sauce.** In small saucepan, melt ¼ cup butter. Remove from heat; stir in flour, salt, pepper and paprika until smooth. Blend in milk.

4. Cook, stirring, over medium heat to boiling point, or until thickened and smooth.
5. In small amount of boiling water, cook potato and carrot 10 minutes; drain.
6. In 2 tablespoons butter, sauté onion until golden – about 5 minutes.
7. In prepared casserole, layer half of the potato and carrot, half the onion and half the salmon or 1 can of tuna. Top with half the sauce. Repeat, layering with potato, carrot, onion, the salmon or tuna and remaining sauce. Dot with 2 tablespoons butter.
8. On lightly floured pastry cloth, roll dough to a 14-by-10-inch oval. With 2½-inch round cookie cutter, cut out three pastry rounds; reserve.
9. Fit oval pastry over salmon-potato mixture. Brush top of pie with some of egg-yolk mixture. Cut reserved pastry rounds in half; arrange on top of pastry as pictured. Brush with egg-yolk mixture. Trim and turn edges under; flute decoratively.
10. Bake 30 to 40 minutes, or until browned and juices bubble through steam vents. Serve warm.
MAKES 8 SERVINGS

SALMON MOUSSE

1 envelope unflavored
  gelatine
½ cup cold water
2 cans (1-lb size) red
  salmon
1½ cups diced peeled
  cucumber

¼ cup lemon juice
½ cup mayonnaise
½ teaspoon salt
6 drops liquid hot-pepper
  seasoning
½ cup heavy cream,
  whipped

1. In small saucepan, sprinkle gelatine over ½ cup cold water; heat over low heat, stirring constantly, until gelatine is dissolved. Set aside.
2. Drain salmon; turn into pie plate. Discard any skin and large bones; flake fish.
3. In electric-blender container, combine about one quarter each of the salmon, cucumber, and lemon juice. Blend at high speed until smooth. Pour into large bowl. Repeat until all is used.
4. Stir in mayonnaise, salt, hot-pepper seasoning and dissolved gelatine. Fold in whipped cream. Turn into 5-cup fish-shape mold or ring mold.
5. Refrigerate until firm – at least 4 hours.
6. To unmold: Run a small spatula around edge of mold; invert over serving platter; shake gently to release. If necessary, place a hot, damp cloth over mold; shake again to release. Garnish with lemon slices and parsley, if desired.
MAKES 6 TO 8 SERVINGS

SAVORY SALMON-TUNA LOAF

1 can (7 oz) chunk-style
  tuna
1 can (7¾ oz) salmon
2 tablespoons butter or
  margarine
2 tablespoons chopped
  onion
1 cup soft white-bread
  crumbs
2 eggs
¾ cup milk

2 tablespoons chopped
  parsley
½ teaspoon salt
½ teaspoon
  Worcestershire sauce
1 tablespoon lemon juice

Sauce
1 can (1 lb) stewed
  tomatoes
1 tablespoon cornstarch

1. Preheat oven to 350F. Grease an 8½-by-4½-by-2½-inch loaf pan. Place a lightly greased strip of foil down center, letting it extend over ends.
2. Drain tuna. Drain salmon; remove skin and bones.
3. In hot butter in small skillet, sauté onion until tender. Stir in bread crumbs. Remove from heat.
4. In medium bowl, slightly beat eggs. Stir in milk, parsley, salt, Worcestershire, and bread-crumb mixture. Fold in tuna, salmon, and lemon juice until well blended. Turn into prepared loaf pan.
5. Bake 45 minutes, or until knife inserted in center comes out clean.
6. **Make Sauce.** Drain ¼ cup liquid from tomatoes into small saucepan. Stir in cornstarch until

dissolved; stir in tomatoes and remaining liquid. Bring to boiling, stirring constantly. Keep warm.
7. Let loaf stand about 3 minutes. Loosen around edges with spatula; holding foil, gently lift loaf onto serving platter, so brown crust is on top. Carefully remove foil. Serve loaf with sauce.
MAKES 6 SERVINGS

TUNA-RONI PILAF

3 tablespoons butter or
  margarine
2 green onions, cut in
  ¼-inch pieces
2 stalks celery, cut in
  ¼-inch pieces
1 green pepper, cut in
  strips

1 pkg (8 oz) chicken-
  flavored rice-and-
  vermicelli mix
1 can (3 oz) sliced
  mushrooms,
  undrained
1 can (2 oz) chopped
  pimiento, undrained
2 cans (7-oz size) solid-
  pack tuna, drained

1. In hot butter in large skillet, sauté onion, celery, and green pepper just until tender – about 5 minutes.
2. Add rice-and-vermicelli mix; cook, stirring, until vermicelli is golden. Stir in water specified on package label, seasoning from the mix, mushrooms, pimiento, and tuna.
3. Bring to boiling; cover; simmer, following package directions, until liquid is absorbed. Stir gently; serve.
MAKES 4 TO 6 SERVINGS

TUNA AND EGGPLANT PARMIGIANA

Tomato Sauce
2 tablespoons butter or
  margarine
½ cup chopped onion
1 clove garlic, crushed
1 can (1 lb, 1 oz) Italian
  tomatoes, undrained
1 can (8 oz) tomato sauce
1 tablespoon sugar
¼ teaspoon salt
¼ teaspoon Italian
  seasoning
¼ cup all-purpose flour

¼ teaspoon salt
⅛ teaspoon pepper
1 medium eggplant
  (about 1¼ lb)
⅓ cup salad oil
2 cans (6½-oz size)
  chunk-style tuna,
  drained and flaked
¼ cup grated Parmesan
  cheese
½ pkg (8-oz size)
  mozzarella cheese,
  sliced

1. **Make Tomato Sauce.** In hot butter in medium saucepan, sauté onion and garlic until onion is golden-brown – about 5 minutes. Add tomatoes, tomato sauce, sugar, ¼ teaspoon salt, and the Italian seasoning; bring to boiling. Reduce heat, and simmer, uncovered and stirring frequently, 20 minutes – there should be about 3 cups.
2. Meanwhile, on sheet of waxed paper, combine flour, ¼ teaspoon salt, and the pepper. Wash egg-

plant; cut crosswise into ½-inch-thick slices. Dip slices into flour mixture, coating both sides.

3. Heat about 2 tablespoons oil in skillet. Add eggplant, a few slices at a time, and sauté until golden-brown on each side. Remove eggplant as it browns. Add more oil as needed.

4. Preheat oven to 350F.

5. Spoon half of sauce into an 8-by-8-by-2-inch or a 9-inch round baking dish. Place half of eggplant in sauce; top with tuna, then remaining eggplant. Spoon remaining sauce over top. Sprinkle with Parmesan cheese; then top with mozzarella slices.

6. Bake, uncovered, 30 minutes, or just until cheese is melted and golden.

MAKES 6 SERVINGS

HOT TUNA BUNS

1 can (7 oz) solid-pack tuna, drained and flaked	⅓ cup mayonnaise or cooked salad dressing
4 stuffed green olives, sliced	3 tablespoons sweet-pickle relish
4 oz Cheddar cheese cubes	2 tablespoons finely chopped onion
3 hard-cooked eggs, coarsely chopped	¼ teaspoon salt
	8 frankfurter rolls

1. Preheat oven to 400F.

2. In medium bowl, combine tuna, olives, cheese, egg, mayonnaise, pickle relish, onion, and salt; mix well.

3. Spoon into rolls. Wrap each in foil. Place on cookie sheet.

4. Bake 10 minutes. Serve hot, right in foil.

MAKES 8 SERVINGS

HERRING IN SOUR CREAM

2 cans (6-oz size) matjes-herring fillets, or 3 matjes-herring fillets	24 whole black peppers
	2 bay leaves
	¾ cup sour cream
1 medium onion	¼ cup sauterne

1. Rinse fillets in cold water; drain; dry on paper towels. Cut crosswise into 1-inch pieces. Then slice onion into thin rings.

2. In medium bowl, layer onion rings, black peppers, bay leaves, and herring pieces.

3. Combine sour cream and wine. Pour over herring mixture, mixing gently to combine.

4. Refrigerate, covered, 8 hours, or overnight.

MAKES 2 CUPS – 6 APPETIZER SERVINGS

Note: Herring in Sour Cream may be stored, covered, in refrigerator 3 days.

PICKLED HERRING

1 whole Iceland salt herring, head and tail removed*	4 to 6 sprigs fresh dill, tied with twine
¾ cup sugar	1 bay leaf
½ teaspoon whole allspice, crushed	1 cup water
1 medium red onion, sliced	1 cup Swedish or white vinegar

1. Rinse herring well. In medium bowl, add cold water to herring to cover. Refrigerate, covered, 24 hours, changing water once. Next day, remove herring from water; dry on paper towels.

2. To fillet herring: Starting from tail end of herring, loosen and peel off skin with sharp paring knife. With head end of herring at right, split herring in half lengthwise, cutting just above center bone. Remove upper half. Carefully cut lower half of herring away from bone. Lift out bones, and discard. You will have 2 fillets.

3. Cut each fillet crosswise into 1-inch pieces.

4. Meanwhile, in medium saucepan, combine sugar, allspice, onion, dill, bay leaf, and 1 cup water. Cook, over medium heat, stirring constantly, until sugar dissolves; bring to boiling. Reduce heat; simmer, uncovered, 5 minutes.

5. With slotted utensil, remove and reserve onion rings; remove and discard dill. Stir in vinegar. Let mixture cool completely.

6. In pint jar with tight-fitting lid, layer herring alternately with onion. Fill jar to top with cooled vinegar mixture; cover. Refrigerate at least 24 hours before using. (Herring may be stored in refrigerator for a week.) Serve as an appetizer.

MAKES 1 PINT – 4 SERVINGS

*Or use 1 can (6 oz) schmaltz-herring fillets; proceed as recipe directs, omitting step 2.

KIPPERED HERRINGS ON TOAST

2 cans (7- to 8-oz size) kippered herrings	Paprika
	1 lemon, cut into wedges
5 white-bread slices, toasted and buttered	

1. Place opened cans of herrings in skillet. Add hot water to come halfway up sides of cans.

2. Cover skillet, and simmer until herrings are hot – about 15 minutes.

3. Remove crusts from toast; cut slices in half.

4. With narrow spatula, carefully remove herrings from cans; arrange on toast halves.

5. Dust kippered herrings with paprika, and garnish each sandwich with a lemon wedge.

MAKES 5 SERVINGS

Shellfish, in some form – fresh, frozen or canned – is available all year long. To most people, even fish haters, it's a delicacy; to dieters, a great boon, because it's low in calories but high in protein.

SHELLFISH

Shellfish	Available as	How to Prepare
Clams	Fresh in shell; Canned whole, minced	Raw, steam, bake
Crabs: blue	Cooked in shell, crabmeat; Canned	Steam, bake, boil
Crabs: Dungeness	Cooked in shell, crabmeat; Canned	
Crabs: king	Frozen legs, crabmeat; Canned	
Lobster	Fresh in shell, lobster meat; Frozen in shell, lobster meat; Canned	Boil, broil
Lobster tails	Frozen in shell	Boil, broil
Oysters	Fresh in shell, shelled in liquid; Frozen; Canned whole or stew	Raw, fry, sauté, poach, bake
Scallops; sea	Fresh; frozen	Sauté, bake, fry, broil
Scallops: bay	Fresh; frozen	Sauté, bake, fry, broil
Shrimp	Fresh in shell, shelled; Frozen in shell, shelled	Boil, broil, fry
Squid	Whole	Raw, boil

CLAMS

*H*ard-shell clams are large and are used for broth and chowder. Soft-shell clams are usually small and are used for steaming and fritters. Clams may be served on the half shell, dipped in cocktail sauce.

MANHATTAN CLAM CHOWDER

4 bacon slices, diced
1 cup sliced onion (about 4)
1 cup diced carrots (about 4)
1 cup diced celery
1 tablespoon chopped parsley
1 can (1 lb, 12 oz) tomatoes
2 jars (11½-oz size) clams

Water
2 teaspoons salt
4 whole black peppercorns
1 bay leaf
1½ teaspoons dried thyme leaves
3 medium potatoes, pared and diced (3½ cups)

1. In large skillet, sauté bacon until almost crisp.
2. Add onion; cook until tender – about 5 minutes.
3. Add carrots, celery, and parsley; cook over low heat 5 minutes, stirring occasionally.
4. Drain tomatoes; reserve liquid in 1-quart measure. Add tomatoes to vegetables in kettle.
5. Drain clams; set clams aside. Add clam liquid to tomato liquid. Add water to make 1½ quarts liquid. Pour into kettle. Add salt, peppercorns, bay leaf, and thyme.

6. Bring to boiling. Reduce heat; cover, and simmer 45 minutes.
7. Add potatoes; cover, and cook 20 minutes.
8. Chop clams; add to chowder. Simmer, uncovered, 15 minutes. Serve hot.
MAKES 8 LARGE SERVINGS

NEW ENGLAND CLAM CHOWDER

2 slices bacon
1 cup finely chopped onion
2 cups cubed pared potato
1 teaspoon salt
Dash pepper
1 cup water

1 pint shucked fresh clams, or 2 cans (10½-oz size) minced clams
2 cups half-and-half
2 tablespoons butter or margarine

1. Chop bacon coarsely. Sauté in large kettle until almost crisp. Add onions; cook about 5 minutes.
2. Add cubed potato, salt, pepper, and 1 cup water. Cook, uncovered, 15 minutes, or until potato is fork-tender.
3. Meanwhile, drain clams, reserving clam liquid. Chop clams coarsely.
4. Add clams, ½ cup clam liquid, the half-and-half, and butter to kettle; mix well. Heat about 3 minutes; do not boil.
MAKES 4 SERVINGS

FRIED CLAMS

1 quart shucked clams
1 egg, slightly beaten
1 teaspoon salt
1/8 teaspoon pepper
Dash paprika

1 cup packaged dry
    bread crumbs
1/2 cup butter or
    margarine

1. Drain clams, reserving 2 tablespoons liquid.
2. Combine clam liquid with egg, salt, pepper, and paprika.
3. Dip clams in egg mixture; then roll in bread crumbs, coating completely.
4. In hot butter in medium skillet, sauté clams 3 to 4 minutes on each side, or until golden. Drain well on paper towels.
MAKES 4 TO 6 SERVINGS

CLAM FRITTERS

1. Make Savory Batter, below.
2. Drain very well, on paper towels, 2 jars (6-oz size) whole clams.
3. Meanwhile, in deep skillet or deep-fat fryer, slowly heat salad oil or shortening (at least 2 inches) to 375F on deep-frying thermometer.
4. Dip clams into batter, coating evenly. Deep-fry a few at a time, turning once, 4 to 5 minutes, or until golden-brown on both sides.
5. Drain well on paper towels.
6. Serve hot with lemon wedges and Sour-Cream Tartar Sauce, page 28.
MAKES ABOUT 25 FRITTERS, OR 5 OR 6 SERVINGS

SAVORY BATTER

1 1/2 cups sifted all-
    purpose flour
2 1/4 teaspoons baking
    powder
3/4 teaspoon salt
1 egg white

2 egg yolks
3/4 cup milk
1 1/2 tablespoons salad oil
1 teaspoon grated lemon
    peel

1. Sift flour with baking powder and salt.
2. In small bowl, with rotary beater, beat egg white until stiff peaks form.
3. In medium bowl, with same beater, beat egg yolks, milk, and salad oil until smooth.
4. Gradually add flour mixture, beating until smooth.
5. Gently fold egg white into batter with grated lemon peel.
MAKES 1 3/4 CUPS

CRABS

*T*he lovely, delicate flavor of crab appeals to almost
    everybody, so much so that crab is the second most
popular shellfish in America. Crabmeat is available in
cans and frozen packages. Even though crabmeat may
seem expensive, there is absolutely no waste, and one
pound serves four adequately.

BOILED CRABS

1/4 cup salt   16 live hard-shell crabs

1. In large kettle, bring 4 quarts water and the salt to boiling.
2. Place crabs in colander; wash in cold water until crabs seem clean.
3. Holding crabs by tongs or back feelers plunge head first into boiling water; return water to boiling. Reduce heat, and simmer, covered, 12 to 15 minutes.
4. Drain; let cool.
5. To remove meat: Twist off claws and legs; crack them with nutcracker or hammer; remove meat.
6. Lay crab on top shell. Insert point of a knife under forward end of the flap that folds under body from rear; break if off, and discard.
7. Pick up crab in both hands; pull upper and lower shells apart. Discard top shell.
8. Hold crab under running water; remove gills and all spongy material.
9. Cut away any hard membrane along outer edge; carefully remove meat with fork.
MAKES ABOUT 2 CUPS CRABMEAT

SAUTÉED SOFT-SHELL CRABS

6 soft-shell crabs
1 egg
1 teaspoon salt
1/8 teaspoon pepper
1/8 teaspoon paprika

1/2 cup packaged dry
    bread crumbs
1/4 cup unsifted all-
    purpose flour
1/2 cup butter or
    margarine

1. To clean crabs: With sharp knife, cut away segment that folds under body from rear; discard.
2. With scissors, remove head, about 3/4 inch behind eyes; discard.
3. Lift back shell on either side; scrape away lungs and spongy substance under it. Wash crabs well under cold running water.
4. Beat egg slightly with salt, pepper, and paprika. Combine bread crumbs with flour.
5. Dip crabs in egg mixture, then in crumb mixture, coating completely.
6. In hot butter in large skillet, sauté crabs until golden – about 4 minutes on each side.
MAKES 3 SERVINGS

SHERRIED CRABMEAT

2 cans (6½-oz size)
  crabmeat
¼ cup butter or
  margarine
3 tablespoons all-
  purpose flour
½ teaspoon salt
Dash pepper
Dash ground red pepper
¾ cup bottled clam juice
½ cup heavy cream
1½ tablespoons dry
  sherry

1 hard-cooked egg, finely
  chopped
1 tablespoon finely
  chopped onion
½ cup sliced fresh
  mushrooms
1 tablespoon finely
  chopped parsley
1 tablespoon finely
  chopped chives
¼ cup packaged dry
  bread crumbs
8 toast slices

1. Drain crabmeat; remove any cartilage.
2. Melt 3 tablespoons butter in medium saucepan.
Remove from heat; stir in flour, salt, and the
peppers, until smooth. Gradually stir in clam juice
and cream.
3. Bring mixture to boiling, stirring; sauce will be
thickened and smooth.
4. Stir in sherry, egg, and crabmeat.
5. Heat rest of butter in small skillet; in it, sauté onion, mushrooms, parsley, and chives until mushrooms are tender – about 5 minutes. Stir in bread
crumbs.
6. Spoon crabmeat mixture over toast slices; top
with mushroom mixture.
MAKES 8 SERVINGS

CRAB MORNAY

1 pkg (10 oz) frozen
  chopped spinach
3 tablespoons butter or
  margarine
2 tablespoons all-
  purpose flour
½ teaspoon salt
Dash ground red pepper
1½ cups milk
½ cup light cream
1 cup grated Swiss
  cheese

1 tablespoon lemon juice
2 cans (6½-oz size)
  crabmeat, drained and
  flaked
¼ cup packaged dry
  bread crumbs
Paprika
4 to 6 buttered-toast
  slices

1. Cook spinach as package label directs; drain.
Place in 1½-quart casserole; set aside.
2. Preheat oven to 375F.
3. Melt butter in medium saucepan. Remove from
heat.
4. Blend in flour, salt, and pepper. Gradually stir in
milk and cream.
5. Bring to boiling, stirring; boil 1 minute.
6. Add cheese; stir until melted. Add lemon juice
and crabmeat.

7. Pour over spinach. Sprinkle with bread crumbs
and paprika.
8. Bake 15 minutes, or until crumbs are browned.
9. Serve on toast.
MAKES 4 TO 6 SERVINGS

SCALLOPED CRAB

1 lb fresh crabmeat, or 2
  cans (6½-oz size)
  crabmeat
½ cup dry sherry
¼ cup butter or
  margarine
2 tablespoons finely
  chopped onion
¼ cup unsifted all-
  purpose flour
½ cup milk

1 cup light cream
1 tablespoon
  Worcestershire sauce
1 teaspoon salt
Dash pepper
2 egg yolks
2 tablespoons butter or
  margarine, melted
½ cup packaged dry
  bread crumbs

1. Preheat oven to 350F. Lightly grease 6 or 8 scallop shells or a 1-quart casserole.
2. Drain crabmeat, removing any cartilage. Sprinkle
crabmeat with ¼ cup sherry; toss to mix well.
3. In ¼ cup hot butter in medium saucepan, sauté
onion until tender – 5 minutes.
4. Remove from heat. Stir in flour. Gradually stir in
milk and cream; bring to boiling, stirring; reduce
heat, and simmer until quite thick – 8 to 10 minutes.
5. Remove from heat; add Worcestershire, salt,
pepper, and rest of sherry. Stir a little of sauce into
egg yolks; return to rest of sauce in saucepan; mix
well. Stir in crabmeat mixture.
6. Turn into shells or casserole.
7. Toss 2 tablespoons butter with crumbs to mix
well. Sprinkle crumbs evenly over crabmeat.
8. Place shells on cookie sheet; bake 20 minutes, or
until mixture is bubbly and crumbs are lightly
browned. (Bake casserole 25 minutes.)
MAKES 6 TO 8 SERVINGS

CRABCAKES

1 lb fresh crabmeat, or 2
  cans (6½-oz size)
  crabmeat
½ cup butter or
  margarine
½ cup finely chopped
  onion
1 cup packaged dry
  bread crumbs

3 eggs, beaten
1 teaspoon salt
1 teaspoon dry mustard
1 tablespoon chopped
  parsley
¼ cup heavy cream
All-purpose flour
Lemon wedges

1. Flake crabmeat. (If using canned crabmeat,
drain; remove any cartilage; then flake.)
2. In ¼ cup hot butter in medium skillet, cook onion
until tender – about 5 minutes.
3. Remove from heat; add bread crumbs, mixing
well.

4. Add crumb mixture to crabmeat along with eggs, salt, mustard, parsley, and cream; mix well.

5. Shape mixture into 8 thick patties, about 2½ inches in diameter. Coat with flour.

6. Heat remaining butter in large skillet. Add patties; sauté until golden on both sides. Serve with lemon wedges.

MAKES 4 SERVINGS

CRÊPES WITH CURRIED CRABMEAT

Crabmeat Filling
5 tablespoons butter or
  margarine
¼ cup unsifted all-
  purpose flour
¾ teaspoon salt
1½ cups milk
1 can (6½ oz) crabmeat,
  drained
1 teaspoon chopped
  shallots or green
  onions
½ cup dry white wine
1 teaspoon curry powder
¼ teaspoon Worcester-
  shire sauce
⅛ teaspoon pepper
Dash ground red pepper

Crepes
1 cup milk
¾ cup sifted all-purpose
  flour
¼ teaspoon salt
2 eggs

Salad oil

Topping
1 egg yolk
⅛ teaspoon salt
4 tablespoons butter or
  margarine, melted
2 teaspoons lemon juice
¼ cup heavy cream,
  whipped

Grated Parmesan
  cheese

1. **Make Crabmeat Filling.** For white sauce, melt 4 tablespoons butter in medium saucepan. Remove from heat. Add flour and ½ teaspoon salt; stir until smooth. Gradually stir in milk; bring to boiling, stirring constantly. Reduce heat; simmer 5 minutes. Remove from heat, and set aside.

2. Separate crabmeat pieces, removing membrane. In 1 tablespoon hot butter in medium skillet, sauté shallots 1 minute. Add crambeat; sauté 2 minutes longer. Add wine, curry, ¼ teaspoon salt, the Worcestershire, and both the peppers; cook over medium heat, stirring 3 minutes. Stir in 1 cup of the white sauce just until blended. Refrigerate while making crepes.

3. **Make Crêpes.** In medium bowl, with rotary beater, beat milk with flour and salt until smooth. Add eggs; beat until well combined.

4. Slowly heat a 5½-inch skillet until a little water sizzles when dropped on it. Brush pan lightly with salad oil. Pour about 1½ tablespoons batter into skillet, tilting pan so batter covers bottom completely.

5. Cook until nicely browned on underside. Loosen edge; turn; cook until browned on other side. Remove from pan; cool on wire rack; then stack on waxed paper. Repeat with rest of batter to make 18 crepes; lightly brush pan with oil before making each.

6. Preheat oven to 350F. Remove filling from refrigerator. Spoon 1 rounded tablespoonful onto each crêpe; fold two opposite sides over filling. Arrange in shallow baking dish; cover with foil. Bake 20 to 25 minutes, or until heated through.

7. Meanwhile, **make Topping:** In small bowl, with rotary beater, beat egg yolk with salt until foamy; gradually beat in 2 tablespoons butter. Mix remaining butter with lemon juice; gradually beat into egg-yolk mixture. With wire whisk or rubber spatula, fold in remaining white sauce just until combined. Fold in whipped cream.

8. Uncover hot crêpes. Spoon topping over them; then sprinkle lightly with grated Parmesan cheese. Broil, 4 to 6 inches form heat, until nicely browned.

MAKES 6 SERVINGS

To prepare ahead of time: Make and fill crêpes as directed; cover with foil, and refrigerate. Make topping, but do not add whipped cream. Refrigerate. To serve: Bake crêpes as directed. Fold the whipped cream into sauce, ready to spoon over the crêpes. Sprinkle with cheese.

CRAB MOUSSE

1 envelope unflavored
  gelatine
¼ cup cold water
¼ cup boiling water
¾ cup heavy cream,
  whipped
½ cup mayonnaise or
  cooked salad dressing

3 tablespoons lemon
  juice
1¼ teaspoons salt
2 cups cooked crabmeat,
  coarsely chopped
Salad greens

1. Sprinkle gelatine over ¼ cup cold water; let stand 5 minutes to soften.

2. Add boiling water; stir until gelatine is dissolved. Set aside to cool.

3. Combine whipped cream, mayonnaise, lemon juice, and salt. Gently fold in cooled gelatine and crabmeat. Turn into 1-quart mold.

4. Refrigerate until firm – about 2 hours.

5. To unmold: Run a small spatula around edge of mold; invert over serving platter; shake gently to release. If necessary, place a hot, damp cloth over mold; shake again to release. Surround with salad greens.

MAKES 6 SERVINGS

LOBSTER

*M*ost elegant of shellfish, lobster is represented in our waters by two kinds. The spiny or rock lobster, without claws and with the meat concentrated in the tail; caught in southern waters. The northern lobster, with claws, caught from Maine to Nova Scotia. Native lobsters can be bought alive or boiled whole; or boiled, removed from shell, then packed in tins or frozen. And don't overlook frozen lobster tails!

BOILED LIVE LOBSTERS

1 lemon, sliced	2 (1-lb size) live lobsters
1 medium onion, sliced	Melted butter or
6 tablespoon salt	margarine
2 bay leaves	Lemon wedges
8 black peppercorns	

1. In deep, 10-quart kettle, combine 6 quarts water, the lemon, onion, salt, bay leaves, and whole black peppercorns. Bring to boiling; then reduce heat, and simmer, covered, 20 minutes.
2. Holding each lobster by the body with tongs, with claws away from you, plunge it into the boiling water. Return to boiling; reduce heat. Cover kettle; simmer lobsters 12 to 15 minutes.
3. Remove lobsters from kettle; place on back. Split body lengthwise, cutting through thin undershell and lobster meat and back shell. Spread open. Remove and discard dark vein and small sac 2 inches below head. Leave in green liver (tomalley) and red roe (coral).
4. Crack large claws, to let excess moisture drain off.
5. Serve lobsters at once, with plenty of melted butter and lemon wedges.
MAKES 2 SERVINGS
To remove meat from shell
1. Lay lobster on back shell; twist off all claws close to body. Slit center of thin shell entire length of lobster. Remove meat from tail in one piece.
2. Lay tail meat red side down. Slit lengthwise down middle; remove and discard dark intestinal vein. Remove meat from body of lobster with pick, discarding stomach (a small sac about 2 inches below head). Green liver (tomalley) may be used if desired.
3. Crack large claws with nutcracker; remove meat.
MAKES 2 SERVINGS

BROILED LOBSTERS

2 (1-lb size) live lobsters	Pepper
Butter or margarine,	Paprika
melted	Lemon wedges
Salt	

1. Kill lobster: Lay lobster on back shell on wooden board. To sever spinal cord, insert point of knife through to back shell where body and tail of lobster come together.
2. With sharp knife, split body of lobster down middle, cutting through thin undershell just to back shell and leaving back shell intact.
3. Discard dark intestinal vein running down center of lobster; also discard small sac below head.
4. Crack large claws. Lay lobsters on back shell on broiler rack; spread open. Brush with melted buter; sprinkle with salt, pepper, and paprika.
5. Broil, 4 inches from heat, 12 to 15 minutes, or until lightly browned. Serve with lemon wedges and melted butter.
MAKES 2 SERVINGS

BROILED ROCK-LOBSTER TAILS

4 (5-oz size) frozen rock-lobster tails, thawed	**Lemon Butter**
	1/2 cup butter or
1/4 cup butter or	margarine
margarine, softened	2 tablespoons lemon
Salt or garlic salt	juice
	1 teaspoon salt
	Dash ground red pepper

1. With kitchen shears, cut undershells away from lobster. Bend each shell backward until it cracks.
2. Place lobster tails, shell side up, on rack in broiler pan. Broil, 6 inches from heat, 5 minutes.
3. Turn lobster tails; spread with soft butter; sprinkle with salt. Broil 5 to 7 minutes longer, or until tender.
4. Meanwhile, heat all ingredients for Lemon Butter in small saucepan, over low heat, stirring, until butter melts. Serve with lobster.
MAKES 4 SERVINGS

BAKED STUFFED LOBSTERS

5 1/2 teaspoons salt	2 tablespoons finely
4 (1 1/2-lb size) live lobsters, or 2 pkg (10-oz size) frozen rock-lobster tails	snipped fresh oregano leaves, or 1 tablespoon dried oregano leaves
	2 tablespoons finely
3/4 cup butter or	snipped parsley
margarine, melted	1/8 teaspoon pepper
1/4 cup finely chopped	1/4 cup light cream
onion	1/4 cup sherry
2 1/4 cups small day-old white-bread cubes, crust removed	1/4 cup grated Parmesan cheese

1. In large kettle, bring to boiling about 5 quarts cold water with 5 teaspoons salt. Plunge lobsters head first into water (water should cover them); bring to boiling again. Reduce heat; simmer, covered, 20 minutes.

2. Run cold water over lobsters. Drain; let cool at room temperature. (If using frozen lobster tails, cook as package label directs. Drain; cool.)

3. In ¼ cup hot butter in small skillet, sauté onion until golden – about 5 minutes. Add to bread cubes in large bowl, along with oregano, parsley, rest of salt, and the pepper; toss with fork until well mixed.

4. Preheat oven to 400F.

5. To remove meat from lobsters: Twist off lobster claws. With nutcracker, crack large claws; remove meat. (Small claws may be saved and used as garnish.)

6. Turn lobsters on backs; with sharp knife or kitchen shears, cut down center from head to tail. Remove and discard membrane; remove and discard small sac, about 2 inches long, just below head. Remove meat with pick. Reserve tomalley (green liver). Remove meat from tail; discard black vein.

7. Cut meat in bite-size pieces. Wash shells, and dry. (If using frozen tails, cut meat in bite-size pieces; wash shells, and dry.)

8. Add lobster meat, with tomalley, to bread mixture, along with cream, sherry, and rest of butter. Toss with fork to combine well. Spoon stuffing into shells. Sprinkle with grated cheese.

9. Place stuffed lobsters in flat baking dish. Cover top of dish with foil; bake 20 to 30 minutes, or until lobsters are thoroughly hot.

MAKES 4 SERVINGS

LOBSTER BISQUE

1 small carrot, sliced	3 (5-oz size) frozen rock-
1 medium onion, peeled	lobster tails, unthawed
and quartered	½ cup butter or
1 teaspoon salt	margarine
2 black peppercorns	3 tablespoons all-
1 bay leaf	purpose flour
Pinch dried thyme leaves	2 cups heavy cream
1 sprig parsley	1 to 2 tablespoons sherry
6 cups water	(optional)
¾ cup dry white wine	Paprika

1. In 4-quart saucepan, combine carrot, onion, salt, peppercorns, bay leaf, thyme, parsley sprig and 6 cups water.

2. Add wine and lobster tails; bring just to boiling. Reduce heat; simmer, covered, 5 minutes.

3. Remove lobster tails from cooking liquid; cool. Continue to cook liquid, uncovered, about 45 minutes, to reduce to about half of original volume. Strain; liquid should measure 2 cups.

4. Melt butter in same saucepan. Remove from heat; stir in flour to make a smooth mixture.

5. Gradually add reserved cooking liquid, stirring until smooth. Bring to boiling, stirring; reduce heat; simmer 10 minutes, stirring occasionally.

6. Meanwhile, remove meat from shells; cut into very small pieces.

7. Gradually add cream, then lobster and sherry. Reheat gently – do not boil. Sprinkle with paprika before serving.

MAKES 5 CUPS; 6 SERVINGS

LOBSTER THERMIDOR

1 small onion, peeled	**Sauce**
and sliced	⅓ cup butter or
½ lemon, sliced	margarine
1 tablespoon salt	¼ cup unsifted all-
5 black peppercorns	purpose flour
1 bay leaf	½ teaspoon salt
5 (6-oz size) frozen rock-	Dash ground mace
lobster tails	¼ teaspoon paprika
2 tablespoons sherry	1½ cups light cream
	1 tablespoon sherry
	½ cup grated sharp
	Cheddar cheese

1. In 6-quart kettle with 3 quarts water, place onion, lemon, 1 tablespoon salt, the peppercorns, and bay leaf; bring to boiling.

2. With tongs, lower frozen lobster tails into boiling mixture; return to boiling. Reduce heat, and simmer, covered, 9 minutes.

3. With tongs or slotted spoon, remove lobster tails from kettle. Set aside until cool enough to handle. Discard the cooking liquid.

4. To remove meat from shells: With scissors, carefully cut away thin undershell, and discard. Then insert fingers between shell and meat, and gently pull out meat in one piece. Wash four shells; dry with paper towels, and set aside.

5. Cut lobster meat into bite-size pieces. Place in medium bowl; toss with 2 tablespoons sherry.

6. Preheat oven to 450F.

7. **Make sauce:** Melt butter in 2-quart saucepan; remove from heat. Stir in flour, salt, mace, and paprika until smooth. Gradually stir in the light cream.

8. Bring to boiling, stirring constantly. Reduce heat, and simmer 2 to 3 minutes. Add lobster meat and sherry; cook over low heat, stirring frequently, until lobster is heated through. Remove from heat.

9. Spoon into shells, mounding it high. Sprinkle with grated cheese and a little paprika, if desired. Place filled shells on cookie sheet. (Prop up tails with crushed aluminum foil to keep them steady.)

10. Bake 10 to 12 minutes, or until cheese is melted and lightly browned. If desired, garnish with lemon wedges and watercress. Serve with fluffy white rice.

MAKES 4 SERVINGS

LOBSTER NEWBURG

3/4 lb cooked lobster meat, or 2 cans (6-oz size) lobster meat
2 egg yolks, slightly beaten
1/2 cup heavy cream
1/4 cup butter or margarine
2 tablespoons sherry
1/2 teaspoon salt
Dash ground red pepper
Dash ground nutmeg

1. If necessary, cut the lobster meat into chunks.
2. Combine egg yolks with cream.
3. Melt butter in medium saucepan, over low heat. Stir in egg mixture and sherry; cook, stirring constantly, until mixture thickens.
4. Remove from heat. Add salt, pepper, nutmeg, and lobster; reheat gently.
5. Serve hot, over buttered toast slices, if desired.
MAKES 3 OR 4 SERVINGS

MUSSELS

MOULES MARINIÈRE

3 dozen mussels
1/2 cup olive oil
1/4 cup chopped onion
1/4 cup chopped celery
2 to 3 cloves garlic, crushed
1 teaspoon dried basil leaves
1/2 cup dry white wine
1 tablespoon lemon juice
1/8 teaspoon pepper
1 teaspoon salt
1 can (1 lb) Italian plum tomatoes, undrained
1/4 cup chopped parsley

1. Check mussels, discarding any that are not tightly closed. Scrub well under cold running water, to remove sand and seaweed. With a sharp knife, trim off the "beard" around edges. Place mussels in large bowl; cover with cold water; let soak 1 to 2 hours.
2. Lift mussels from water, and place in a colander. Rinse with cold water; let drain.
3. In olive oil in 6-quart kettle, sauté onion, celery, garlic and basil, stirring, until golden and tender — about 10 minutes. Add wine, lemon juice, pepper, salt, undrained tomatoes and half of parsley; break up tomatoes with spoon. Bring to boiling.
4. Add mussels; cook over high heat, covered, 5 to 8 minutes, or until shells open. Shake kettle frequently, so mussels will cook uniformly.
5. With slotted utensil, remove mussels to heated serving dish. Keep warm.
6. Spoon sauce over mussels; sprinkle with remaining parsley. Serve immediately.
MAKES 3 OR 4 MAIN-DISH SERVINGS, 6 APPETIZER SERVINGS

OYSTERS

Each variety has a slightly different flavor and shape. Oysters are marketed in their shells, out of their shells, canned or frozen. Probably the most popular way of serving them is on the half shell, with lemon juice and black pepper.

OYSTERS ROCKEFELLER

Rock salt
25 oysters in the shell
3/4 cup butter or margarine
1/4 cup finely chopped onion
1/4 cup finely chopped celery
1/4 cup finely chopped parsley
1/4 clove garlic, finely chopped
1/2 cup packaged dry bread crumbs
1/2 cup finely chopped watercress, packed (no stems)
1/2 cup finely chopped raw spinach, packed (no stems)
Dash anise
1/4 teaspoon salt
1/8 teaspoon liquid hot-pepper seasoning
Lemon wedges (optional)

1. Begin by preheating oven to 450F.
2. In each of 5 large ramekins, or in a large, shallow roasting pan, place a layer of rock salt about 1/2 inch deep.
3. Sprinkle the salt lightly with water, to dampen. Place in oven to preheat while preparing oysters and vegetables.
4. Shuck the oysters (or have oysters shucked at fish market). Drain oysters. Place one on the deep half of each of the oyster shells; discard the other half.
5. In 1/4 cup hot butter or margarine in medium skillet, sauté onion, celery, parsley, and garlic until onion is golden and celery is tender — about 5 minutes.

6. Add rest of butter and crumbs; stir, over medium heat, till butter is melted.

7. Add chopped watercress and spinach, anise, salt, and liquid hot-pepper seasoning; cook, stirring, for 1 minute.

8. Pour off any liquid from oysters. Spread each with 1 tablespoon vegetable mixture, covering oysters completely.

9. Arrange 5 oysters on salt in each ramekin, or place all in roasting pan.

10. Bake, uncovered, about 10 minutes, or just until the oysters curl around the edges. Be careful not to overbake.

11. Serve right in ramekins, or remove to serving plates. Garnish with wedges of lemon, if desired. Serve as a first course or a light supper.

Makes 5 servings

OYSTER STEW

2 pints fresh oysters in liquid, or 2 dozen oysters and 2/3 cup liquid	1/2 teaspoon celery salt
	1/8 teaspoon pepper
	2 cups light cream
	1 cup milk
1/4 cup butter or margarine	Paprika
	Chopped parsley
1/2 teaspoon salt	Oyster crackers

1. Drain oysters, reserving liquid.

2. Heat butter in 3-quart saucepan. Add oysters; cook 3 to 5 minutes, or until edges begin to curl.

3. Add salt, celery salt, pepper, cream, milk, and oyster liquid. Heat, over medium heat, just until bubbles form around edge of pan. Do not boil.

4. Sprinkle with paprika and the chopped parsley. Serve with oyster crackers.

Makes 4 to 6 servings

FRIED OYSTERS

Salad oil or shortening for frying	1/2 teaspoon salt
2 eggs, beaten	1/2 teaspoon pepper
1/4 cup liquid from oysters	3 dozen fresh oysters
	Cracker crumbs

1. In large, heavy skillet, heat salad oil (at least 1 inch) to 375F on deep-frying thermometer.

2. Combine eggs, liquid from oysters, salt, and pepper.

3. Dip oysters in cracker crumbs, then in egg mixture, coating completely.

4. Fry, a few at a time, until golden on both sides — about 3 minutes in all.

5. Drain well on paper towels.

Makes 4 to 6 servings

SCALLOPS

Two varieties are known to American diners. Happily, one kind or the other is obtainable, fresh or frozen, all year long. The tiny bay scallop, tender and delicately flavored, is favored by gourmets. The larger sea scallop is more generally available. Both are delicious.

BROILED SEA SCALLOPS

1 lb sea scallops	Salt
1/4 cup butter or margarine, melted	Pepper
	Paprika
1 tablespoon lemon juice	

1. Rinse scallops. Drain; dry on paper towels.

2. Arrange scallops on broiler rack. Combine butter and lemon juice; brush half of mixture over scallops. Sprinkle with salt, pepper, and paprika.

3. Broil, 5 inches from heat, 3 minutes.

4. Turn scallops; brush with remaining lemon-butter mixture. Broil 2 to 3 minutes longer, or until scallops are tender. Serve garnished with parsley sprigs, if desired.

Makes 3 or 4 servings

SCALLOPS WITH MUSHROOMS

1 1/2 lb bay scallops (1 1/2 pints)	1/4 cup unsifted all-purpose flour
1/4 cup butter or margarine	1 1/2 cups milk
	2 teaspoons salt
1/2 lb fresh mushrooms, thinly sliced	Dash pepper
	Dash ground red pepper
1/4 cup chopped green pepper	2 canned pimientos, chopped
	1/4 cup sherry

1. Wash scallops in cold water; drain.

2. Place scallops in large skillet; add water to cover; bring to boiling. Reduce heat, and simmer, uncovered, 2 to 3 minutes, or until scallops are tender. Drain, and set aside.

3. In same skillet, in hot butter, cook mushrooms and green pepper 5 minutes, stirring occasionally.

4. Remove from heat. Blend in flour; then add milk, salt, and peppers. Bring to boiling, stirring.

5. Remove from heat. Add pimientos, sherry, and scallops; reheat gently. Serve hot over toast.

Makes 6 servings

SAUTÉED SCALLOPS

2 lb sea scallops
6 tablespoons butter or
  margarine
2 tablespoons chopped
  shallot

3 tablespoons dry
  vermouth or dry white
  wine
2 tablespoons chopped
  parsley
Lemon wedges

1. Rinse scallops gently under cold water; drain. If large, cut in half.
2. In hot butter in large, heavy skillet, sauté shallot 2 minutes. Add scallops in a single layer (do half at a time, if necessary). Sauté, over medium heat and stirring occasionally, until browned and cooked through – 5 to 8 minutes.
3. With slotted spoon, remove to heated platter; keep warm.
4. Add vermouth and parsley to skillet; heat, over low heat, stirring to dissolve browned bits, until bubbling – about 1 minute. Pour over scallops.
5. Garnish with lemon wedges and with additional parsley, if desired.
MAKES 6 SERVINGS

SCALLOPS PROVENÇAL

1 lb bay or sea scallops
2 tablespoons lemon
  juice
½ lb fresh mushrooms
2 lb fresh tomatoes, or 1
  can (1 lb) whole
  tomatoes, drained
5 tablespoons olive or
  salad oil
4 shallots, sliced

4 parsley sprigs,
  chopped
1 small clove garlic,
  crushed
½ teaspoon salt
Dash white pepper
½ teaspoon dried thyme
  leaves
½ teaspoon dried
  oregano leaves

1. In medium bowl, toss scallops with lemon juice.
2. Wipe mushrooms; slice lengthwise, right through stem, about ⅛ inch thick. Toss with scallops.
3. If using fresh tomatoes, scald in boiling water; peel; remove seeds; chop pulp coarsely.
4. In 2 tablespoons hot oil in 8-inch skillet with tight-fitting cover, sauté half of shallot and parsley with the garlic just until golden. Add tomato, salt, pepper, thyme, and oregano. Cook, covered, over low heat, 20 minutes, stirring occasionally to break up tomatoes. Uncover, and cook for 5 more minutes.
5. In 3 tablespoons hot oil in large skillet, sauté remaining shallot and parsley, stirring, about 5 minutes. Add scallops and mushrooms; cook, uncovered, over high heat 10 minutes, shaking pan and stirring frequently.
6. Stir in tomato mixture; cook 2 minutes longer. Serve at once.
MAKES 6 FIRST-COURSE SERVINGS. OR SERVE TO 4 WITH RICE, AS A MAIN COURSE

SHRIMP

Most popular shellfish is the shrimp, and we eat about ten times as many shrimp as any other shellfish. Our chief source of supply is the Gulf Coast. Shrimp can be bought green or raw (uncooked and unshelled); cooked, in the shell; cooked, deveined, without the shell; in cans; uncooked, frozen; or partially prepared for cooking, then frozen. You can't beat our shrimp dishes.

SHRIMP IN GARLIC BUTTER
(Scampi)

2 lb large, unshelled raw
  shrimp
½ cup butter or
  margarine
½ cup salad or olive oil

¼ cup chopped parsley
6 cloves garlic, crushed
1 teaspoon salt
Dash ground red pepper
¼ cup lemon juice

1. Rinse shrimp; remove shells, leaving tails on. Devein (using a small, sharp knife, slit each shrimp down back; lift out sand vein). Wash under cold running water. Drain; pat dry with paper towels.
2. Melt butter in shallow broiler pan, without rack, or 13-by-9-by-2-inch baking pan. Add salad oil, 2 tablespoons parsley, the garlic, salt, pepper, and lemon juice; mix well.
3. Add shrimp, tossing lightly in butter mixture to coat well. Arrange in single layer in pan.
4. Broil, 4 to 5 inches from heat, 5 minutes. Turn shrimp; broil 5 to 10 minutes longer, or until lightly browned.
5. Using tongs, remove shrimp to heated serving platter. Pour garlic mixture over all, or pour it into a small pitcher, to pass.
6. Sprinkle shrimp with remaining chopped parsley. Garnish platter with lemon slices, if you wish.
MAKES 8 SERVINGS
Note: Shrimp may be baked at 400F for 8 to 10 minutes, or just until tender, instead of broiled.

GRILLED SHRIMP IN THE SHELL

2 lb large unshelled raw
  shrimp
½ cup butter or
  margarine
4 cloves garlic, crushed

2 tablespoons kosher
  salt
3 tablespoons chopped
  parsley

1. Wash shrimp under cold water; break off feelers, leaving shrimp in shell. Place in large bowl.
2. Melt butter in small saucepan or skillet. Stir in garlic. Pour over shrimp. Sprinkle with salt and 1 tablespoon parsley; toss until shrimp are well coated.
3. To cook on outdoor grill: Place on grill 4 inches above hot coals. Grill 7 minutes; turn; grill 7 minutes longer, or until shrimp are pink and shells are

browned. To cook indoors: Place on rack of broiler pan; broil, 4 inches from heat, 6 minutes on each side, or until golden-brown.

4. Serve at once, sprinkled with remaining parsley. MAKES 6 SERVINGS

SHRIMP VICTORIA

¼ cup butter or margarine	1 tablespoon all-purpose flour
1 lb raw shrimp, shelled and deveined	1 teaspoon salt
¼ cup chopped onion	Dash pepper
½ cup sliced fresh mushrooms	1½ cups sour cream

1. In hot butter in large skillet, cook, stirring occasionally, shrimp and onion until shrimp are almost tender – about 5 minutes.

2. Add mushrooms; cook, stirring occasionally, 5 minutes.

3. Remove from heat. Stir in flour, salt, and pepper, mixing well; then stir in sour cream.

4. Reheat gently; do not boil. Delicious served over rice or hot buttered toast.

MAKES 4 SERVINGS

SHRIMP AND VEGETABLES WITH QUICK AÏOLI

Vegetables
3 zucchini (1 lb)	1 tablespoon salt
3 summer squash (1 lb)	
1 small cauliflower (1½ lb)	**Quick Aïoli Sauce**
	2 cups mayonnaise
1 teaspoon salt	3 cloves garlic, crushed
½ teaspoon dried thyme leaves	1 tablespoon lemon juice
	Dash ground red pepper
1 clove garlic, halved	1 tablespoon capers, drained
1 lb raw medium-size shrimp, shelled and deveined	Cherry tomatoes

1. **Prepare Vegetables.** Wash zucchini and summer squash; trim ends. Cut lengthwise into thirds; cut into 2½-inch pieces. Wash cauliflower; cut into flowerets.

2. In large skillet, add 1 teaspoon salt, thyme and 1 halved garlic clove to 1½ inches of water; bring to boiling. Add zucchini, summer squash and cauliflower. Bring to boiling; cook, covered, 1 minute, or just until blanched. Do not overcook.

3. Drain vegetables well; refrigerate.

4. Cook shrimp: In medium saucepan, bring to boiling 2 cups water and 1 tablespoon salt. Add shrimp; return to boiling. Reduce heat; simmer, covered, 3 to 5 minutes, or until shrimp are tender.

5. Drain; refrigerate, covered.

6. **Make Quick Aïoli Sauce.** In small bowl, combine mayonnaise, garlic, lemon juice and pepper. Refrigerate, tightly covered.

7. To serve: Alternate zucchini and summer squash, in groups of four, around edge of chilled serving dish. Set bowl of sauce in center; sprinkle with capers. Arrange cauliflower around bottom of bowl. Garnish with cherry tomatoes. Serve shrimp in a bowl. Serve Aïoli Sauce over shrimp and vegetables.

MAKES 8 SERVINGS

CREOLE SHRIMP-AND-CRAB SOUP

1 sweet red pepper	⅛ teaspoon dried thyme leaves
1 green pepper	
2 carrots	¼ teaspoon ground turmeric
5 medium tomatoes (2 lb), or 1 can (1 lb, 12 oz) whole tomatoes, undrained	1 whole bay leaf
	¼ teaspoon crushed dried hot red pepper
1 white onion, peeled	Water
4 whole cloves	1 teaspoon salt
2 shallots, peeled	1 lb unshelled raw shrimp
2 cans (10¾-oz size) condensed chicken broth, undiluted	1 can (6½ oz) crabmeat, drained and cartilage removed
1½ cups chopped celery	¼ cup lemon juice
½ teaspoon dried basil leaves	1 tablespoon chopped parsley

1. Wash peppers; remove ribs and seeds; cut into small pieces. Pare carrots; slice thinly crosswise – about 1 cup each of pepper and carrot.

2. If using fresh tomatoes, scald in boiling water; peel; remove and discard seeds; chop pulp coarsely. Break up canned tomatoes with fork.

3. Stud the onion with cloves. Slice shallots.

4. In large saucepan, bring 3 cups water and the chicken broth to boiling; add red and green pepper, carrot, tomato, onion with cloves, shallot, celery, basil, thyme, turmeric, bay leaf, and dried red pepper. Bring back to boiling; reduce heat, and simmer, uncovered, 30 minutes.

5. Meanwhile, cook shrimp: In small saucepan, bring 2 cups water with the salt to boiling. Add shrimp; cook over medium heat, uncovered, 10 minutes. Drain, reserving 1 cup cooking liquid. Cool shrimp; remove shells, and devein.

6. Add shrimp, reserved cooking liquid, crabmeat, and lemon juice to soup; cook gently, uncovered, 10 minutes. Add parsley at end of cooking time. Taste, and add salt, if desired.

MAKES 2 QUARTS; 6 TO 8 SERVINGS

SHRIMP CURRY

Curry Sauce

3 tablespoons butter or
  margarine
1 cup chopped onion
1 cup chopped pared
  apple
1 clove garlic, crushed
2 to 3 teaspoons curry
  powder
1/4 cup unsifted all-
  purpose flour
1 teaspoon salt
1/4 teaspoon ground
  ginger
1/4 teaspoon ground
  cardamom
1/4 teaspoon pepper

2 cans (10³/4-oz size)
  condensed chicken
  broth, undiluted
2 tablespoons lime juice
2 teaspoons grated lime
  peel

2 lb raw shrimp, shelled
  and deveined (18 to 20
  per pound)
1 tablespoon salt
1 small onion, peeled
  and sliced
1/2 lemon, sliced
5 black peppercorns
1/4 cup chopped chutney

1. **Make Curry Sauce.** In hot butter in large skillet, sauté chopped onion, chopped apple, garlic, and curry powder until the onion is tender – will take about 5 minutes.
2. Remove from heat; blend in flour, 1 teaspoon salt, the ground ginger, cardamom, and pepper.
3. Gradually stir in chicken broth, lime juice, and grated lime peel.
4. Bring to boiling, stirring constantly. Reduce heat, and simmer sauce, uncovered, 20 minutes, stirring it occasionally.
5. Meanwhile, cook shrimp: Rinse shrimp under cold running water.
6. In a large saucepan, combine 1 quart water, 1 tablespoon salt, the sliced onion, sliced lemon, and black peppercorns; bring to boiling. Add the cleaned shrimp.
7. Return to boiling; reduce heat, and simmer shrimp, uncovered, 5 to 10 minutes, or just until they are tender when tested with a fork.
8. Drain shrimp, discarding cooking liquid. Add shrimp to curry sauce; stir in chopped chutney. Heat gently just to boiling.
9. Serve the Shrimp Curry hot, with Curry Accompaniments and Fluffy White Rice, below.
MAKES 6 SERVINGS

Curry Accompaniments:

Chutney
Pickled watermelon rind
Chopped green pepper
Chopped green onion
Diced avocado
Cucumber slices
Diced tomato
Salted nuts
Peanuts
Sliced banana
Raisins
Pineapple chunks

FLUFFY WHITE RICE

3 cups cold water
1 1/2 cups long-grain white
  rice
1 1/2 teaspoons salt
1 1/2 tablespoons butter or
  margarine

1. In heavy, medium-sized saucepan with tight-fitting cover, combine 3 cups cold water with the rice, salt, and butter.
2. Bring to boiling, uncovered.
3. Reduce heat; simmer, covered, 15 to 20 minutes, or until rice is tender and water is absorbed.
4. Fluff up with fork.
MAKES 4 1/2 CUPS

BATTER-FRIED SHRIMP

Mustard Sauce

1/2 cup sour cream
1/4 cup prepared mustard
2 tablespoons prepared
  horseradish
1/8 teaspoon liquid hot-
  pepper seasoning
1 1/2 teaspoons salt

Salad oil or shortening
  for deep-frying

Batter

1 1/2 cup sifted all-
  purpose flour
2 1/4 teaspoons baking
  powder
3/4 teaspoon salt
3/4 teaspoon curry
  powder
1 egg white
2 egg yolks
1 1/2 tablespoons salad oil
3/4 cup milk

1 1/2 lb large raw de-
  veined, shelled shrimp

1. **Make Mustard Sauce.** In medium bowl, combine sour cream with rest of sauce ingredients. Refrigerate, covered, at least 1 hour, or until serving time.
2. In electric skillet or deep-fat fryer, slowly heat oil (1 1/2 to 2 inches) to 375F on deep-frying thermometer.
3. **Make Batter.** Sift flour with baking powder, salt, and curry powder.
4. In small bowl, with rotary beater, beat egg white until stiff; set aside. With same beater, beat egg yolks with salad oil and milk. Gradually beat in flour mixture until smooth. Fold in egg white.
5. Dip shrimp into batter to coat well. Fry shrimp, 6 at a time, 2 or 3 minutes on each side, or until golden-brown all over.
6. Lift from fat with slotted spoon; drain on paper towels. Keep warm while frying rest.
7. Serve with Mustard Sauce.
MAKES 3 OR 4 SERVINGS

SEAFOOD SAUCES

APRICOT SAUCE

½ cup pineapple juice
2 to 4 tablespoons dry mustard
2 tablespoons soy sauce
1 cup apricot jam
2 teaspoons grated lemon peel
¼ cup lemon juice

1. In medium skillet, stir pineapple juice into mustard until mixture is smooth.
2. Add remaining ingredients. Heat, stirring, over low heat, until jam is melted.
MAKES ABOUT 1¾ CUPS

CUCUMBER SAUCE

1 cup sour cream
1 cup grated pared cucumber
¼ teaspoon salt
Dash pepper
¼ teaspoon onion salt
¼ teaspoon paprika
½ teaspoon Worcestershire sauce
1 teaspoon lemon juice
Dash liquid hot-pepper seasoning

1. In medium bowl, combine all ingredients, mixing well.
2. Refrigerate until serving.
MAKES ABOUT 2 CUPS

PORTUGUESE SAUCE

2 cans (1-lb size) stewed tomatoes
1 cup finely chopped onion
4 teaspoons Worcestershire sauce
2 teaspoons salt
⅛ teaspoon pepper
2 tablespoons cornstarch
¼ cup water

1. In medium saucepan, combine tomatoes and onion; cook, covered, over low heat, until onion is tender – about 20 minutes. Stir in Worcestershire, salt, and pepper.
2. In small bowl, combine cornstarch with ¼ cup water; stir to mix well. Then add to the tomato mixture.

3. Bring to boiling. Reduce heat, and simmer, uncovered, 10 minutes, stirring occasionally. Set aside, and keep warm.
MAKES 2½ CUPS

MUSHROOM SAUCE

1 can (3 oz) chopped mushrooms
About ⅔ cup milk
1 tablespoon butter or margarine
1 tablespoon all-purpose flour
1½ teaspoon salt
¼ teaspoon pepper
1 egg, beaten
3 tablespoons sherry

1. Drain mushrooms, reserving liquid. Add milk to measure 1 cup.
2. Melt butter in small saucepan or in top of double boiler. Remove from heat. Stir in flour. Slowly add milk mixture, stirring until smooth.
3. Bring to boiling, stirring. Reduce heat, and simmer 1 minute. Add salt, pepper, and mushrooms.
4. Stir some of hot mixture into beaten egg. Return to saucepan; cook, stirring, over low heat, until slightly thickened – about 2 minutes. Stir in sherry.
5. Serve at once, or keep warm over hot water.
MAKES ABOUT 1½ CUPS

LEMON-CHIVE SAUCE

⅓ cup butter or margarine
2 tablespoons finely chopped chives
1 tablespoon lemon juice
1 teaspoon grated lemon peel
½ teaspoon salt
Dash pepper

1. Melt butter in small saucepan. Add remaining ingredients.
2. Beat thoroughly. Serve sauce hot. Delicious served over baked or broiled salmon, swordfish, or sole.
MAKES ABOUT ½ CUP

HOLLANDAISE SAUCE

3 egg yolks
6 tablespoons butter or margarine, melted
1/3 cup boiling water or boiling fish stock
2 tablespoons lemon juice
1/4 teaspoon salt
Dash ground red pepper

1. In top of double boiler, with wire whisk, slightly beat egg yolks.
2. Slowly stir in butter. Gradually add water, beating constantly.
3. Cook, stirring, over barely simmering water (water in double-boiler base should not touch pan above), just until thickened.
4. Remove double-boiler top from hot water. Gradually beat lemon juice, salt and pepper into sauce.
5. Cover and keep hot over warm water until serving.
MAKES ABOUT 1 CUP

LEMON SOUR-CREAM SAUCE

1 1/2 tablespoons lemon juice
1 cup sour cream
1 teaspoon grated lemon peel
2 tablespoons snipped chives

1. Combine all ingredients in small bowl.
2. Mix well. Serve along with fish.
MAKES 1 CUP

SEAFOOD-COCKTAIL SAUCE

1/2 cup chili sauce
1 tablespoon prepared horseradish
1 tablespoon lemon juice
2 teaspoons Worcestershire sauce
1/4 teaspoon salt
Dash ground red pepper

1. In small bowl, combine all ingredients; mix well. Refrigerate, covered, at least 3 hours.
2. Serve with cold boiled shrimp, crabmeat, or lobster.
MAKES 2/3 CUP

RÉMOULADE SAUCE

1 cup mayonnaise
1 tablespoon chopped onion
1 tablespoon chopped parsley
1 tablespoon chopped celery
2 tablespoons Dijon-style mustard
1 tablespoon prepared horseradish
1 teaspoon paprika
1/2 teaspoon salt
Dash liquid hot-pepper seasoning
1/4 cup salad oil
1 tablespoon vinegar
1/2 teaspoon Worcestershire sauce

1. Combine all ingredients in small bowl; mix until well blended.
2. Refrigerate several hours or overnight.

3. Serve with cold boiled shrimp, crabmeat, lobster, or with tomatoes.
MAKES 1 1/2 CUPS

TARTAR SAUCE

1 cup mayonnaise or cooked salad dressing
1/3 cup drained sweet-pickle relish
1 tablespoon lemon juice
1 tablespoon drained capers
1 tablespoon chopped parsley
1 teaspoon grated onion
1/8 teaspoon salt

1. Combine all ingredients; mix well.
2. Refrigerate, covered, until well chilled – at least 2 hours.
MAKES 1 1/3 CUPS

SOUR-CREAM TARTAR SAUCE

1 cup sour cream
2 tablespoons sweet-pickle relish, drained
1/2 teaspoon salt
Dash liquid hot-pepper seasoning
1 teaspoon grated onion

1. Thoroughly combine all ingredients in a small bowl.
2. Refrigerate until well chilled. Serve with shrimp or clam fritters.
MAKES ABOUT 1 CUP

PARSLEY BUTTER

1/4 cup butter or margarine
2 tablespoons chopped parsley
1 tablespoon snipped chives

1. In small bowl, let butter soften slightly. Beat until smooth.
2. Mix in parsley and chives until well blended.
3. Turn out onto waxed paper; shape into a bar about 6 by 3/4 by 3/4 inches. Refrigerate or place in freezer 1 hour, or until hard.
4. Cut into 6 pieces. Serve on chicken, chops, steaks, hamburgers.
MAKES 6 SERVINGS

QUICK MUSTARD SAUCE

1/2 cup mayonnaise or cooked salad dressing
1 teaspoon chopped onion
1/2 cup prepared mustard

1. Combine all ingredients; mix well.
2. Refrigerate, covered, until ready to use.
MAKES ABOUT 1 CUP

Poultry

So plentiful and usually such a good buy any time of the year, poultry is company food at family prices – a good thing to remember if you have to do much entertaining and your budget is limited. Of course chicken is the all-time champ of the poultry clan, but don't neglect those others: duckling, Rock Cornish game hen, turkey, goose. You'll find them all here.

CHICKEN

Chicken boiled or broiled, chicken roasted or fried, is tender, undemanding food. Cook it with wine as the French so often do, and you have a sophisticated treat. Or with oregano, like the Italians; with orange-almond sauce, like the Chinese; with paprika, as the Hungarians do; with curry, East Indian style. It's easy to do almost anything with chicken, we do believe, except ruin it. Just try any of the fascinating recipes that follow. But first there are some things you should know . . .

Selection and Storage
When you buy chicken, choose your market for cleanliness. A good market keeps fresh chicken refrigerated and frozen chicken frozen at all times. The birds we buy in our markets today are the most carefully chaperoned in the world. Since January, 1959, virtually all chickens have passed a rigid processing-plant inspection by officials of the U.S. Department of Agriculture. All water and equipment used in processing must also be officially checked. Today, chickens are one of our safest, most carefully controlled foods.

Look for the government inspection mark on wing tags, outer wrappers, boxes, or giblet wrappers. If you do not see the mark on the chicken or its wrapping, check with your retailer. Most fresh, ice-packed chickens are shipped from the processor in large wooden boxes, which carry the inspection stamp. Although you will not find a mark on these chickens, you may be sure they traveled to your market in an adequately stamped crate.

How much should you buy? The figures below are amounts to buy for each serving:

Broiling	½ of one 1½-pound broiler
Frying	¾ pound
Roasting	¾ pound
Stewing	¾ pound

Remember these figures mean *per serving*, not per person served. Gauge your needs by the appetites of those eating. If you expect them to take seconds, figure how many servings you need, not how many people you will feed. Also, if yours is a dark-meat family, take advantage of legs and thighs sold separately. One whole chicken plus several legs will give each his choice.

Often, fresh ready-to-cook poultry arrives at the market in a plastic wrapping, which it wears right into your kitchen. If so, leave it in this wrapping, and keep it in the refrigerator until you are ready to cook it. Today's safe, clean packaging means these birds can be kept under refrigeration for several days or even a bit longer. If your butcher cuts up your chicken or wraps it whole in his own wrapping, or if you buy parts, remove the butcher's wrappings when you get home. Rewrap loosely in foil, waxed paper, or plastic wrap, and keep refrigerated until used. Use within a few days.

If you buy frozen chicken or packaged frozen parts, keep frozen until 24 hours before cooking. Then unwrap, and leave it in the food compartment of the refrigerator overnight. Or, for quicker defrosting, unwrap, and thaw in cold running water for 1 to 2 hours.

Test Your Terminology

Broiler or broiler-fryer: A chicken about 9 weeks old, weighing 1½ to 3½ pounds. Tender, with smooth-textured skin and flexible breastbone cartilage. Of all chickens sold, 70 to 80 per cent are broiler-fryers.

Roaster: Tender chicken of 3½ to 5 pounds, about 12 weeks old.

Fryer: Same as broiler, but used to mean the largest of the broilers, usually weighing over 2½ pounds.

Stewing chicken: Mature female chicken, less tender than roaster. Can be broiler chicken allowed to grow old or layer past the ideal age for laying eggs.

Capon: Desexed (through surgery) male chicken, weighing 4 to 8 pounds. Very tender, with large amount of white meat.

Ready-to-cook or oven-ready: All commericially produced birds are now sold ready to cook. Pinfeathers are removed, hair singed, bird thoroughly cleaned inside and out; giblets cleaned, wrapped, and placed in cavity; bird shipped to market in iced wooden crates in refrigerated trucks.

New methods of feeding, distribution, and marketing have made the following terms obsolete:

Drawn: Dressed poultry with entrails, head, feet removed. All inspected poultry is shipped this way.

Milk-fed: Fed rations high in milk to increase fat, bleach skin, soften muscle. Obsolete, since all poultry get milk by-products daily.

Spring chickens: Young cockerel chickens, once sold in spring as by-product of egg industry.

TIMETABLE FOR ROASTING STUFFED CHICKEN

(Chicken and dressing should be at room temperature)

Chicken	Ready-to-cook weight	Oven temperature	Approximate roasting time
Broiler-fryer	3 lb	375F	1½ hours
Roaster	4 lb	325F	3½ hours
Capon	5 lb	325F	2½ hours
	8 lb	325F	4½ hours

ROAST STUFFED CHICKEN

4-lb roasting chicken

Bread Stuffing
¼ cup butter or margarine
⅔ cup finely chopped onion
1 chicken liver, chopped
1⅓ cups white-bread cubes
¼ cup chopped parsley
½ teaspoon dried thyme leaves
½ teaspoon salt
Dash pepper
¼ cup milk

2 tablespoons butter or margarine, melted
1 can (13¾ oz) chicken broth

1. Wash chicken well under cold running water; dry with paper towels. Remove and discard excess fat.
2. Preheat oven to 325F.
3. **Make Stuffing.** In ¼ cup hot butter in medium skillet, sauté onion until golden. Add liver; sauté 1 minute.
4. Remove from heat; stir in bread cubes, parsley, thyme, salt and pepper. Add milk, tossing mixture with a fork.
5. Fill body cavity with stuffing; close with poultry pins. Tie legs together with twine. Tuck wings under body. Reserve rest of giblets for use another time.
6. Place chicken on rack in shallow roasting pan. Brush with melted butter. Roast, uncovered, 3 hours, or until leg joints move easily; baste occasionally with pan drippings.
7. Remove chicken to heated platter; remove poultry pins and twine. Let stand 15 minutes before carving.
8. Skim fat from drippings. Add chicken broth to pan. Cook over medium heat, stirring to dissolve browned bits; simmer until reduced to 1 cup. Strain into gravy boat.
MAKES 4 TO 6 SERVINGS

ROAST CHICKENS WITH HERB-MUSHROOM STUFFING

2 (2½-lb size) broiler-fryers
½ cup butter or margarine, melted
1 tablespoon finely chopped onion
1½ cups coarsely chopped fresh mushrooms
3 cups grated day-old white-bread crumbs
2 tablespoons finely snipped parsley
2 tablespoons coarsely snipped fresh marjoram leaves*
2 tablespoons finely snipped fresh chives
½ teaspoon salt
⅛ teaspoon pepper
⅛ teaspoon ground nutmeg

Gravy
3 tablespoons all-purpose flour
1½ cups canned chicken broth
1 tablespoon corasely snipped fresh marjoram leaves*
½ teaspoon salt
⅛ teaspoon pepper

1. Rinse broiler-fryers inside and out under running cold water. Dry well with paper towels.

2. Preheat oven to 325F.

3. In ¼ cup hot butter in medium skillet, sauté onion and mushrooms until tender – about 5 minutes.

4. In large bowl, with fork, lightly toss sautéed vegetables and bread crumbs with rest of ingredients, except remaining melted butter, until well mixed. Loosely fill neck and body cavities of broiler-fryers.

5. Truss each chicken: Bring skin over neck opening; fasten to back with skewer. Close cavity with skewers. Bend wings under body. Tie legs together at ends.

6. Place chickens, breast side up, on rack in shallow, open roasting pan. Brush with some of melted butter. Cover loosely with foil.

7. Roast 2 to 2½ hours. Remove foil last half hour, and brush chickens with rest of butter.

8. Place on heated platter; remove skewers. Keep warm while making gravy.

9. **Make Gravy.** Drain all but 3 tablespoons drippings from roasting pan. Add flour; stir to make a smooth paste. Gradually stir in chicken broth.

10. Add rest of gravy ingredients; bring to boiling, stirring. Mixture will be thickened and smooth. Simmer, stirring, 1 minute longer.

11. Serve gravy hot, with chicken and stuffing.

MAKES 4 TO 6 SERVINGS

* Or substitute dried herbs for fresh, using half the quantity.

CHICKEN BASQUAISE

5-lb roasting chicken, with giblets	½ teaspoon dried tarragon leaves
¼ cup butter or margarine, softened	¼ teaspoon crushed dried hot red pepper
2 teaspoons dried tarragon leaves	2 sprigs parsley
2 teaspoons dried oregano leaves	10 small white onions, peeled
1 teaspoon salt	2 shallots, sliced
⅛ teaspoon pepper	1 large green pepper, sliced
1 can (13¾-oz) chicken broth	1 large red pepper, sliced
1 teaspoon salt	¼ cup unsifted all-purpose flour
½ teaspoon dried oregano leaves	

1. Preheat oven to 350F.

2. Wash chicken inside and out under cold running water; also wash chicken giblets. Dry on paper towels.

3. Combine softened butter with 2 teaspoons tarra-gon and 2 teaspoons oregano. Put half of butter mixture and the liver in cavity of chicken.

4. Rub outside of chicken with rest of butter mixture. Sprinkle with 1 teaspoon salt and pepper.

5. Place chicken in shallow, 15-by-10-inch roasting pan without rack. Roast 2 hours, basting several times with pan drippings.

6. About 30 minutes before chicken is done, cook vegetables: In 11-inch skillet with tight-fitting cover, bring chicken broth, salt, oregano, tarragon, red pepper, rest of giblets and parsley to boiling.

7. Add onions and shallot; cook, covered, over medium heat 15 minutes. Remove and discard giblets and parsley.

8. Layer green and red pepper over onions; cook, covered, 15 minutes, or just until vegetables are tender. Drain, reserving liquid; add water, if necessary, to make 2 cups.

9. In small saucepan, combine ¾ cup pan drippings with flour; mix well. Stir in reserved vegetable liquid. Bring to boiling, stirring. Serve as sauce.

10. Serve vegetables with chicken.

MAKES 4 TO 6 SERVINGS

SWEET-AND-SOUR CHICKEN

2 whole chicken legs and 2 whole chicken breasts	1 cup sugar
	2 tablespoons cornstarch
½ cup all-purpose flour	¾ cup cider vinegar
⅓ cup salad oil or shortening	1 tablespoon soy sauce
1 teaspoon salt	¼ teaspoon ground ginger
¼ teaspoon pepper	1 chicken-bouillon cube
	1 large green pepper, cut in ½-inch-wide strips

Sauce
1 can (13½ oz) pineapple chunks

1. Wash chicken; pat dry with paper towels. Coat chicken with flour.

2. Heat oil in large skillet. Add chicken, a few pieces at a time, and brown on all sides. Remove as browned to shallow roasting pan, arrange pieces skin side up. Sprinkle with salt and pepper.

3. Meanwhile, preheat oven to 350F.

4. **Make Sauce.** Drain pineapple chunks, pouring syrup into 2-cup measure. Add water to make 1¼ cups.

5. In medium saucepan, combine sugar, cornstarch, pineapple syrup, vinegar, soy sauce, ginger and bouillon cube; bring to boiling, stirring constantly. Boil 2 minutes. Pour over chicken.

6. Bake, uncovered, 30 minutes. Add pineapple chunks and green pepper; bake 30 minutes longer, or until chicken is tender.

MAKES 4 SERVINGS

ROAST CAPON PARMIGIANA

5½-to-6-lb ready-to-cook capon
Salt
Pepper
½ teaspoon dried rosemary leaves
1 celery stalk, cut up
1 garlic clove, peeled and quartered
1 large onion, quartered
2 tablespoons butter or margarine, softened
1 cup mayonnaise
2 tablespoons lemon juice
1 cup grated Parmesan cheese
1 can (10¾ oz) condensed chicken broth, undiluted
½ cup water
3 tablespoons all-purpose flour

1. Preheat oven to 400F.
2. Wash capon well, inside and out, under cold water. Pat dry inside and out with paper towels. Sprinkle inside with 1 teaspoon salt, ¼ teaspoon pepper and the rosemary. Rinse giblets; place in roasting pan.
3. Fill body cavity with celery, garlic and onion. Tie legs together; fold wing tips under back. Skewer skin at neck. Spread butter over capon. Insert thermometer inside thigh at thickest part.
4. Roast, uncovered, 1 hour. Reduce oven temperature to 325F; roast, basting with butter in pan, 1 hour, or until meat thermometer registers 185F and leg moves easily at joint.
5. Remove capon from oven. Combine mayonnaise and lemon juice; spread over entire surface of capon. Sprinkle with Parmesan cheese.
6. Return to oven; continue roasting 10 minutes, or until golden and crusty.
7. Remove capon to heated platter. Remove string. Let stand 20 minutes.
8. Meanwhile, make gravy: Pour undiluted chicken broth into roasting pan; bring to boiling, stirring to dissolve brown bits. Strain into a 2-cup measure; skim off and discard fat.
9. In small saucepan, stir ½ cup water into flour until flour is dissolved. Add chicken broth. Bring to boiling, stirring constantly, until mixture thickens; reduce heat; simmer 5 minutes. Add salt and pepper, if necessary.
10. Garnish capon with buttered rice, peas and carrots. Pass gravy.
MAKES 8 SERVINGS

Chicken Stew with Vegetables, recipe on page 41
Roast Cornish Hens au Vin Blanc, recipe on page 57
Roast Capon Parmigiana

*F*ried chicken can be crisp and delicate and easy to digest, or it can be greasy, heavy, and utterly unattractive. With our simple recipe, you'll make it perfectly and often – no doubt about that! One thing about fried chicken – it's right, no matter what the occasion; cold at your next picnic, for instance; hot, at an important company dinner, with your best china and silver.

Incidental tips: *Have a supply of paper bags and paper towels, if you plan to fry chicken often. The bags, to simplify flouring the chicken; the paper towels, to dry the chicken well, so that flour or bread crumbs or batter or whatever will adhere to it.*

GOLDEN-FRIED CHICKEN

3-to-3¹/₂-lb broiler-fryer, cut up	¹/₄ teaspoon pepper
¹/₃ cup all-purpose flour	Salad oil or shortening (about 1¹/₄ cups)
1¹/₂ teaspoons salt	

1. Wash chicken pieces under cold running water. Thoroughly dry with paper towels. Fold under wing tips.
2. In clean bag, combine flour, salt, and pepper. Add chicken to bag, a few pieces at a time, and shake to coat evenly with flour mixture.
3. In electric skillet, pour in salad oil, or melt shortening, to measure one fourth inch; heat at 375F. (Or slowly heat oil or shortening in large skillet with tight-fitting cover.)
4. Add chicken, a few pieces at a time, starting with meatiest pieces; brown on all sides, turning with tongs. Remove pieces as they are browned. It takes about 20 minutes to brown all the chicken.
5. Carefully pour off all but 2 tablespoons fat from skillet.
6. Using tongs, return chicken to skillet, placing pieces skin side down. Reduce temperature to 300F, or turn heat low. Cook, covered, 30 minutes. (If using electric skillet, leave steam vent open.) Then turn chicken skin side up, and cook, uncovered, 10 minutes, or until meat is fork-tender and skin is crisp.
7. Remove chicken to heated platter, or place in napkin-lined basket. Serve at once.
MAKES 4 SERVINGS

PERFECT FRIED CHICKEN

2¹/₂-to-3-lb broiler-fryer, cut into serving pieces	³/₄ cup cornflake crumbs
¹/₃ cup evaporated milk, undiluted	2 teaspoons salt
³/₄ cup unsifted all-purpose flour	¹/₄ teaspoon pepper
	Salad oil

1. Wash chicken under cold water; dry on paper towels.
2. Pour milk into large pie plate; dip chicken into milk.
3. In a clean paper bag, combine flour, cornflake crumbs, salt and pepper. Then shake chicken, a few pieces at a time, in crumb mixture in the bag, coating well.
4. Pour salad oil to depth of ¹/₄ inch in two (8-inch) skillets. Heat slowly. Brown chicken lightly, turning once with tongs.
5. Cover; reduce heat; cook 40 to 45 minutes, turning occasionally to insure even browning.
6. Remove covers; cook 5 minutes longer, to crisp the crust.
MAKES 4 SERVINGS

SESAME FRIED CHICKEN

2¹/₂-to 3-lb broiler-fryer, cut in serving pieces	2 teaspoons salt
¹/₃ cup evaporated milk, undiluted	¹/₄ teaspoon pepper
¹/₂ cup unsifted all-purpose flour	1 teaspoon paprika
	¹/₄ cup sesame seed
	Salad oil or shortening

1. Wipe chicken well with damp paper towels.
2. Dip in milk in shallow dish. Then roll in flour combined with rest of ingredients, except salad oil.
3. In each of two medium skillets, slowly heat salad oil (at least ¹/₄ inch deep) until a drop of water sizzles when added to hot oil.
4. Brown chicken pieces on both sides, turning with tongs.
5. Reduce heat; cook covered, 40 to 45 minutes, or until tender.
6. Remove covers; cook 5 minutes longer. Drain well on paper towels.
MAKES 4 SERVINGS

GARLIC CHICKEN

3¹/₂-lb broiler-fryer, cut in serving pieces	1 teaspoon salt
¹/₄ cup butter or margarine	8 cloves garlic, crushed
	¹/₂ cup chopped parsley

1. Wash chicken pieces; pat dry with paper towels.
2. In hot butter, in large, heavy skillet, brown chicken pieces on both sides.
3. Remove from heat; sprinkle chicken with salt and garlic.
4. Cook, covered, over low heat, about 40 minutes, or until chicken is tender. Sprinkle parsley over chicken.
5. Serve chicken with sauce spooned over.
MAKES 4 SERVINGS

CHICKEN PAPRIKASH

2 (2-lb size) broiler fryers,
  quartered
1/4 cup butter or
  margarine
2 1/4 teaspoons salt
1/4 teaspoon pepper
Paprika
1 can (10 3/4 oz)
  condensed chicken
  broth, undiluted

Giblets (gizzard, heart)
  and neck
10 small white onions,
  peeled
8 small carrots, pared
1/4 cup unsifted all-
  purpose flour
1/4 cup water
1 cup sour cream
1 tablespoon chopped
  parsley

1. Rinse chicken well; dry with paper towels.
2. In hot butter in Dutch oven, brown chicken pieces well, turning with tongs, on all sides – about 30 minutes.
3. When browned, sprinkle with salt, pepper and 1 tablespoon paprika. Add chicken broth, giblets and neck. (Reserve liver for another use.) Add onions and carrots. Place a large sheet of waxed paper just under the lid. Pour off any liquid that collects on top of paper during cooking, to keep it from diluting sauce.
4. Bring to boiling; reduce heat; simmer gently, covered, about 1 hour, or until chicken and vegetables are tender.
5. Remove chicken and vegetables to heated casserole; cover loosely with foil; keep warm.
6. Remove giblets; chop fine; set aside. Discard neck.
7. In small bowl, blend flour with 1/4 cup water to make a smooth paste. Stir into hot liquid in Dutch oven until smooth.
8. Bring to boiling, stirring; reduce heat and simmer 2 minutes, or just until sauce has thickened slightly.
9. Remove from heat. Slowly stir in chopped giblets and sour cream; heat gently, but do not boil as the sour cream may curdle.
10. To serve: Pour sauce over chicken and vegetables. Sprinkle with parsley.
MAKES 6 SERVINGS

CHICKEN IN BUTTERMILK

3-to-3 1/2-lb roasting
  chicken, cut in 8
  pieces
1 tablespoon salad oil
1 tablespoon butter or
  margarine
1/3 cup chopped onion
1 can (1 lb) tomatoes,
  drained

1/2 teaspoon salt
1/8 teaspoon white pepper
1/2 teaspoon sugar
1 cup buttermilk
1/4 cup snipped chives
1/4 cup chopped dill or
  parsley

1. Wash chicken under cold water; dry well on paper towels. Heat oil and butter in 4-quart Dutch oven or large, heavy skillet.
2. In hot oil, sauté chicken pieces and onion, turning the chicken until browned all over, 10 to 15 minutes.
3. Add tomatoes, salt, pepper, sugar and buttermilk. Stir to combine. Simmer, covered, 25 to 30 minutes. Add chives and dill; cook, uncovered, 5 minutes longer.
MAKES 4 SERVINGS

CHICKEN À LA KING

4-lb roasting chicken, cut
  up
5 cups water
2 teaspoons salt
1/4 teaspoon pepper
1 medium onion
1 medium carrot
3 parsley sprigs

Sauce
1/4 cup butter or
  margarine
2 tablespoons grated
  green pepper

1/2 lb fresh mushrooms,
  thickly sliced
1/4 cup all-purpose flour
1 teaspoon salt
2 cups broth from
  chicken
1 cup light cream or
  half-and-half
1 egg yolk
1 canned pimiento, cut in
  strips

4 slices white toast,
  halved diagonally

1. Wash chicken and giblets under cold water. Wipe with paper towels. Place in 6-quart Dutch oven with 5 cups water, 2 teaspoons salt, the pepper, onion, carrot and parsley.
2. Bring to boiling; reduce heat and simmer gently, covered, 1 hour, or until tender. Remove chicken from broth; reserve broth (you will need 2 cups).
3. Remove chicken from bones in large pieces; cut into uniform pieces, about 1 1/2 inches. Chicken should measure 3 1/2 cups. (Reserve giblets for use another time.)
4. **Make Sauce.** In hot butter in large skillet, sauté green pepper and mushrooms, stirring, over low heat 5 minutes.
5. Remove from heat; stir in flour and salt; then gradually stir in chicken broth and light cream until smooth. Bring to boiling, stirring; simmer, stirring, 5 minutes, or until thickened.
6. Stir a small amount of hot mixture into egg yolk, mixing well. Pour back into hot sauce; cook a few minutes. Add chicken and pimiento strips; cook gently 5 minutes, or until hot.
7. Turn into serving dish. Arrange toast points around edge.
MAKES 6 SERVINGS

Clockwise from top right:
Coq au Vin with New Potatoes, recipe on page 40 • Chicken Basquaise, recipe on page 31
Poached Chickens with Vegetables, recipe on page 40 • Chicken Breasts Florentine, recipe on page 43

OVEN-FRIED CHICKEN WITH CUMBERLAND SAUCE

2¹/₂-b broiler-fryer, cut in serving pieces	**Cumberland Sauce**
¹/₂ teaspoon salt	³/₄ cup currant jelly
Dash pepper	¹/₄ cup orange juice
¹/₄ cup unsifted all-purpose flour	1 teaspoon dry mustard
¹/₄ cup butter or margarine, melted	¹/₈ teaspoon ground ginger

1. Preheat oven to 375F. Grease a 2-quart, shallow baking dish.
2. Wash chicken thoroughly in cold water; pat dry with paper towels.
3. In a clean paper bag, combine salt, pepper, and flour. Shake chicken pieces, a few at a time, in flour mixture until well coated.
4. Arrange chicken in baking dish; pour on butter. Cover with lid or foil; bake 30 minutes.
5. Meanwhile, **make Cumberland Sauce:** In small saucepan, combine sauce ingredients; bring to boiling. Remove from heat; stir until smooth.
6. At end of baking period, remove cover from chicken. Pour on sauce; bake 30 minutes longer, basting occasionally.
MAKES 3 SERVINGS

OVEN-BARBECUED CHICKEN

2 tablespoons salad oil	¹/₄ teaspoon dry mustard
¹/₂ cup chopped onion	1¹/₄ teaspoons salt
1 cup tomato catsup	¹/₄ teaspoon ground red pepper
2 tablespoons vinegar or ¹/₄ cup lemon juice	¹/₄ teaspoon black pepper
1 tablespoon brown sugar	¹/₄ teaspoon celery seed
1 tablespoon Worcestershire sauce	3 (2-lb size) broiler-fryers, halved
	¹/₂ cup sliced onion

1. Make barbecue sauce: In hot oil in medium saucepan, over medium heat, sauté chopped onion, stirring, until golden – about 5 minutes.
2. Add catsup, 1 cup water, the vinegar and brown sugar; simmer, covered, 20 minutes.
3. Stir in Worcestershire, mustard, salt, red and black peppers, and celery seed. Simmer, covered, 10 minutes longer. Makes 2 cups.
4. Preheat oven to 375F. Wash chicken; pat dry with paper towels.
5. Place chicken, skin side up, in large shallow roasting pan (18 by 12 inches). Brush with barbecue sauce. Arrange sliced onion over top.
6. Bake, uncovered and basting occasionally with the barbecue sauce, 1 hour and 15 minutes, or until tender.
7. Serve chicken with remaining barbecue sauce.
MAKES 6 SERVINGS

POACHED CHICKEN WITH CUCUMBER

4-lb roasting chicken	¹/₂ teaspoon dried rosemary or thyme leaves
2 large tomatoes (1 lb)	
Boiling water	¹/₈ teaspoon pepper
2 medium carrots (¹/₃ lb), pared, thinly sliced	2 cans (10³/₄-oz size) condensed chicken broth, undiluted
2 medium onions (¹/₂ lb), peeled, thinly sliced	2 large cucumbers (1 lb)
1 bay leaf	Chopped parsley
1 teaspoon salt	

1. Preheat oven to 350F.
2. Wash chicken and giblets; dry with paper towels. Remove excess fat.
3. Peel tomatoes: Dip each into boiling water 1 minute; lift out with slotted utensil; peel off skin. Cut one tomato in half; remove seeds; chop coarsely.
4. In 6-quart Dutch oven, combine giblets, carrot, onion, bay leaf and chopped tomato. Cook over medium heat 5 minutes, stirring occasionally.
5. In small bowl, combine salt, rosemary and pepper. Sprinkle chicken inside and out with herb mixture. Tie legs together.
6. Place chicken, breast side up, on top of vegetables. Pour 1 can of chicken broth over vegetables.
7. Poach chicken, uncovered, 1³/₄ hours. Every 15 minutes during first hour, turn chicken; baste with pan liquid.
8. Meanwhile, pare cucumbers; halve lengthwise; remove and discard seeds. Cut each cucumber half into four strips.
9. In small saucepan, bring to boiling remaining can of chicken broth. Add cucumber; simmer, uncovered, 10 to 15 minutes, or until tender. Drain; reserve ¹/₂ cup liquid.
10. Remove chicken and giblets to platter. Remove and discard bay leaf. Skim fat from drippings. Make sauce: Turn drippings, vegetables except cucumbers and ¹/₂ cup liquid into blender or food processor; blend until smooth.
11. To serve: Remove twine from chicken legs. Cut remaining tomato into quarters. Arrange tomato and cucumber around chicken, as pictured. Pour ¹/₂ cup sauce over chicken breast; sprinkle with chopped parsley. Serve remaining sauce with chicken.
MAKES 8 SERVINGS

Poached Chicken with Cucumber ▶

COQ AU VIN WITH NEW POTATOES

2 (2½-lb size) broiler-
   fryers, quartered
6 slices bacon, diced
2 tablespoons butter or
   margarine
8 small white onions,
   peeled
8 small whole
   mushrooms
⅔ cup sliced green onion
1 clove garlic, crushed
2 tablespoons all-
   purpose flour

1 teaspoon salt
⅛ teaspoon pepper
¼ teaspoon dried thyme
   leaves
2 cups Burgundy
1 cup canned chicken
   broth
8 small new potatoes,
   scrubbed
Chopped parsley

1. Day before, wash chickens and pat dry with paper towels.

2. In a 5- or 6-quart oval Dutch oven, over medium heat, sauté bacon until crisp. Remove from Dutch oven; drain on paper towels.

3. Add butter to bacon drippings; heat. In hot fat, brown chicken quarters well on all sides. Remove chicken when browned, and set aside.

4. Pour off all but 2 tablespoons fat from Dutch oven. Add white onions, mushrooms, green onion and garlic to Dutch oven. Over low heat, cook, covered and stirring occasionally, 10 minutes.

5. Remove from heat; stir in flour, salt, pepper and thyme. Gradually add Burgundy and chicken broth; bring mixture to boiling, stirring.

6. Remove from heat. Add potatoes, chicken and bacon to Dutch oven; mix well. Cover Dutch oven and refrigerate overnight.

7. The next day, about two hours before serving time, preheat oven to 400F.

8. Bake coq au vin, covered, about 1 hour and 50 minutes, or until chicken and potatoes are tender.

9. Sprinkle with chopped parsley before serving.
MAKES 6 TO 8 SERVINGS

POACHED CHICKENS WITH VEGETABLES

2 (2½-b size) broiler-
   fryers with giblets
Salt
⅛ teaspoon pepper
¼ cup butter or
   margarine
4 leeks
1½ lb medium carrots,
   pared
1½ lb small new
   potatoes, pared

¼ cup butter or
   margarine, melted
2 tablespoons all-
   purpose flour
1 can (10¾ oz)
   condensed chicken
   broth, undiluted
Watercress
Chopped chives or
   parsley

1. Remove giblets from chickens; rinse giblets, and set aside on paper towels. Rinse chickens well; dry with paper towels. Sprinkle insides of each chicken with 1 teaspoon salt and the pepper. Tuck wings under body; tie legs together. If necessary, fasten skin at neck with a skewer.

2. In ¼ cup hot butter in a oval, 6-quart Dutch oven, brown chickens well all over – takes about 30 minutes. Turn chickens carefully with two wooden spoons; do not break skin. Drain off fat.

3. Meanwhile, coarsely chop giblets. Wash leeks well; cut off roots and discard. Reserve 2 cups chopped top leaves, and add to giblets. Then halve leeks lengthwise, and set aside.

4. Place giblet-leek mixture under browned chickens.

5. Arrange carrots around chicken; simmer, covered, 40 to 50 minutes, or until chickens are tender. Remove from heat.

6. Meanwhile, cook potatoes in 1 inch boiling salted water in medium saucepan, covered, 20 to 25 minutes, or until tender. Drain; then drizzle with 2 tablespoons melted butter.

7. Also, cook halved leeks in 1 inch boiling salted water in medium saucepan, covered, 10 minutes, or until tender. Drain, and drizzle with 2 tablespoons melted butter.

8. Carefully remove chickens to a heated platter, and keep warm in low oven.

9. Simmer carrots, covered, 10 minutes longer, or until tender. Strain drippings; return to Dutch oven. Stir in flour until smooth. Gradually stir in chicken broth; bring to boiling. Reduce heat and simmer 3 minutes. Taste, and add salt, if needed.

10. To serve: Arrange potatoes, carrots, leeks and bunches of watercress around chickens. Sprinkle potatoes with chives or parsley. Pass gravy.
MAKES 4 TO 6 SERVINGS

OLD-FASHIONED CHICKEN AND DUMPLINGS

4-lb roasting chicken, cut
   up
5 cups cold water
½ cup chopped onion
2 teaspoons salt
1 bay leaf
6 black peppercorns

1 large carrot, pared and
   sliced
Dumplings, right
3 tablespoons all-
   purpose flour
3 tablespoons water

1. Wipe chicken pieces with damp paper towels. Place in 6-quart Dutch oven with 5 cups water. Add onion, salt, bay leaf, peppercorns and carrot. Bring to boiling; reduce heat and simmer, covered, 1¼ hours, or until tender.

2. Let chicken cool in broth. Mince giblets fine; add to broth or use another time. Meanwhile, make Dumplings.

3. Remove chicken from broth; measure broth – there should be 5 cups. (If necessary, boil, uncovered, to reduce to 5 cups; or add water or canned chicken broth to measure 5 cups if there is not enough.)

4. Meanwhile, combine flour with 3 tablespoons water in small bowl. Stir to dissolve flour.

5. Stir flour mixture into broth in Dutch oven. Return chicken pieces to broth. Bring to boiling, stirring; drop dumpling batter by rounded tablespoonfuls onto chicken in broth, making 12 to 14 dumplings. Bring to boiling; simmer, covered, 10 to 15 minutes, or until dumplings have risen and cooked through.
6. Serve chicken and dumplings with gravy.
MAKES 6 TO 8 SERVINGS

DUMPLINGS

2 cups sifted all-purpose flour	2 tablespoons chopped green onion
2 teaspoons baking powder	¼ cup butter or margarine
¼ teaspoon salt	¾ cup milk
Dash pepper	

1. In large bowl, sift flour with baking powder, salt and pepper. Stir in onion.
2. With pastry blender or two knives, cut shortening into the flour mixture until it resembles coarse cornmeal. With a fork, stir in the milk until mixture forms a ball and leaves side of bowl.
3. Drop onto chicken as directed in Step 5 of Old-Fashioned Chicken and Dumplings.
MAKES 12 TO 14

BROWN CHICKEN FRICASSEE

5 lb chicken parts (legs, thighs, breasts, wings), or 5-lb stewing chicken, cut up	1½ teaspoons salt
	8 whole allspice
	1 bay leaf
	½ cup light cream
¼ cup butter or margarine	¼ cup unsifted all-purpose flour
1 can (13¾ oz) chicken broth	Chopped parsley
Water	4 cups cooked white rice or mashed potato

1. Wash chicken under cold water; dry on paper towels. Cut legs and thighs apart, if necessary.
2. In hot butter in 6-quart Dutch oven, brown chicken pieces, half at a time, turning with tongs.
3. Pour drippings into a 1-quart measure. Skim fat from top; add chicken broth and enough water to drippings to make 4 cups.
4. Pour back into Dutch oven, along with chicken. Add salt, allspice and bay leaf. Bring to boiling, stirring. Reduce heat and simmer, covered, 1½ hours, or until tender.
5. Remove cooked chicken to heated serving platter; keep warm in low oven.
6. Bring liquid in Dutch oven to boiling. Boil, uncovered, to reduce to 3 cups – about 15 minutes.
7. In small bowl, gradually add light cream to flour, stirring until smooth. Stir into hot broth in Dutch

oven. Cook, stirring, until thickened – about 5 minutes. Strain.
8. Pour some of sauce over chicken. Sprinkle with parsley. Pass rest of sauce with rice or mashed potato.
MAKES 6 TO 8 SERVINGS

CHICKEN STEW WITH VEGETABLES

4-lb roasting chicken, cut into eight pieces	Water
	1 can (8 oz) tomatoes
⅓ cup all-purpose flour	3 carrots (½ lb), halved and pared
2 teaspoons salt	
¼ teaspoon pepper	¼ lb snow peas
1 teaspoon dried thyme leaves	
	Potato Border
2 tablespoons butter or margarine	Instant mashed potato for 6 or 7 servings
2 tablespoons salad oil	¼ cup butter or margarine
8 medium onions, peeled (1¼ lb)	2 teaspoons salt
1 bay leaf	Milk

1. Wash chicken pieces; pat dry with paper towels.
2. In a clean bag, combine flour, salt, pepper and thyme. Shake chicken, four pieces at a time, to coat well. Reserve flour mixture for later use (see Step 7).
3. Heat butter and oil in 6-quart Dutch oven. Add chicken pieces, four at a time, and brown well on all sides. Remove as browned.
4. Add onions to drippings in Dutch oven. Cook, covered, about 5 minutes, or until lightly browned.
5. Return chicken pieces to Dutch oven; add bay leaf, 1½ cups water, the tomatoes and carrots; stir to combine. Place a large sheet of waxed paper just under the lid. Pour off any liquid that collects on paper during cooking, to keep it from diluting sauce. Bring to boiling; reduce heat; simmer, covered, 40 minutes, or until chicken and vegetables are tender when pierced with a fork.
6. Snip off stem ends of snow peas; pull strings. Add peas to chicken stew the last 5 minutes.
7. Combine reserved flour mixture with ¼ cup water; stir into chicken mixture. Remove and discard bay leaf.
8. Simmer, covered, 10 minutes, or until slightly thickened. Turn into large oval baking dish (3-quart).
9. **Make Potato Border.** Prepare mashed potato as package label directs, using the amount of water specified on the package and adding ¼ cup butter, 2 teaspoons salt and the milk called for.
10. Spoon mashed potato into pastry bag with large star tip. Make potato ruching around edge of baking dish. Broil, 6 inches from heat, until potato is lightly browned – about 8 minutes.
MAKES 8 SERVINGS

JAMBALAYA

2½-to-3-lb broiler-fryer, quartered	2 cloves garlic, crushed
¼ cup butter or margarine	1 teaspoon dried thyme leaves
4 sweet Italian sausages, halved crosswise (½ lb)	¼ teaspoon chili powder
	1 can (16 oz) tomatoes
	1 can (13¾ oz) chicken broth
1½ cups ham cubes (cut in 1-inch squares)	1½ teaspoons salt
1 cup sliced onion	¼ teaspoon black pepper
1 cup cut-up green pepper (in 1-inch squares)	1 cup long-grain white rice
	2 tablespoons chopped parsley

1. Wipe chicken pieces with damp paper towels. In hot butter in 6-quart Dutch oven, brown chicken, turning, until golden-brown all over – 15 to 20 minutes. Remove chicken.

2. In drippings in pan, sauté sausage until browned all over; remove. Add ham cubes, and sauté until browned; remove. Preheat oven to 350F.

3. To same drippings, add onion, green pepper, garlic, thyme and chili powder; cook, stirring, about 5 minutes. Add tomatoes, chicken broth, salt, pepper and rice; mix well. Add chicken, sausage and ham; stir to combine. Bring to boiling.

4. Bake, covered, 1 hour, or until chicken and rice are cooked and most of liquid is absorbed.

5. Serve right from pot, or turn into large serving dish. Sprinkle with chopped parsley.

MAKES 6 SERVINGS

CHICKEN TETRAZZINI

2 lb whole chicken breasts, split	3 teaspoons salt
3 lb chicken legs and thighs	⅛ teaspoon ground nutmeg
3 celery tops	Dash ground red pepper
3 parsley sprigs	1 quart milk
2 medium carrots, pared and sliced	4 egg yolks
1 onion, quartered	1 cup heavy cream
2 teaspoons salt	½ cup dry sherry
10 black peppercorns	
1 bay leaf	1 pkg (1 lb) thin spaghetti
Sauce	2 tablespoons butter or margarine
¾ cup butter or margarine	½ lb fresh mushrooms, sliced
¾ cup all-purpose flour	1 lb sharp Cheddar cheese, grated (4 cups)

1. Wash chicken. In a 6-quart kettle with 3 cups water, place the chicken, celery, parsley, carrot, onion, 2 teaspoons salt, the peppers and bay leaf. Bring to boiling; reduce heat and simmer, covered, 1 hour, or until chicken is tender.

2. Remove chicken from stock to bowl; set aside. Strain stock; return to kettle. Bring to boiling; boil gently, uncovered, until reduced to 2 cups – about 30 minutes.

3. Remove chicken meat from bones in large pieces – there should be about 6 cups. Set chicken meat aside.

4. **Make Sauce.** Melt ¾ cup butter in large saucepan. Remove from heat; stir in flour, salt, nutmeg and pepper until smooth. Gradually stir in milk and the 2 cups stock; bring to boiling, stirring constantly. Boil gently, stirring constantly, 2 minutes, or until slightly thickened.

5. In small bowl, beat egg yolks with cream. Gently beat in a little of the hot mixture. Return to saucepan; cook over low heat, stirring constantly, until sauce is hot – do not let it boil. Remove from heat. Add sherry.

6. Cook spaghetti as package label directs; drain. Meanwhile, in hot butter in large skillet, sauté mushrooms, stirring until tender. Return spaghetti to kettle. Add 2 cups sauce, and toss until well combined.

7. Remove another 2 cups sauce and refrigerate, covered. To remaining sauce, add cut-up chicken and the sautéed mushrooms.

8. Divide spaghetti into two 12-by-8-by-2-inch baking dishes, arranging it around edges. Spoon half of chicken mixture into center of each. Sprinkle 2 cups cheese over spaghetti in each dish. Cover with foil, and refrigerate; or bake at once.

9. About 1 hour before serving, preheat oven to 350F. Bake, covered, 30 to 45 minutes, or until piping hot.

10. Just before serving, reheat reserved sauce, and spoon over spaghetti.

MAKES 12 SERVINGS

PÂTÉ-STUFFED CHICKEN BREASTS

1 medium onion, sliced	Water
1 celery stalk, sliced	4 (12-oz size) chicken breasts, split
1 carrot, sliced	2 cans (4¾-oz size) liver pâté
1 parsley sprig	
1 teaspoon salt	1 env unflavored gelatine
¼ teaspoon dried thyme leaves	1 cup heavy cream
1 small bay leaf	Pitted black olives, sliced
1 can (10¾ oz) condensed chicken broth, undiluted	Pimiento-stuffed olives, sliced
	Watercress sprigs

1. In 6-quart kettle, combine onion, celery, carrot, parsley, salt, thyme, bay leaf, undiluted chicken broth, 1⅓ cups water and the chicken breasts; bring to boiling.

2. Reduce heat, and simmer, covered, 30 minutes, or just until chicken breasts are fork-tender.

3. Remove kettle from heat. Let chicken breasts cool in the broth.

4. Remove chicken breasts from broth; reserve broth. Remove skin and bone from chicken breasts; trim edges evenly.

5. On underside of each chicken breast, spread about 1 tablespoon liver pâté, mounding it slightly. Refrigerate chicken breasts, covered, for 1 hour.

6. Meanwhile, strain broth; skim off fat. Reserve 2 cups broth.

7. Make glaze: In medium saucepan, bring reserved broth to boiling. Reduce heat; simmer, uncovered, 30 minutes, or until liquid is reduced to 1 cup.

8. In ¼ cup cold water in medium bowl, let gelatine stand 5 minutes to soften. Add hot broth, stirring to dissolve gelatine.

9. Add heavy cream, mixing until well combined with gelatine mixture.

10. Set bowl with gelatine mixture in ice water; let stand about 20 minutes, or until well chilled but not thickened. Stir occasionally. Remove from ice water.

11. Place chicken breasts, pâté side down, on wire rack; set rack on tray. Spoon glaze over chicken breasts.

12. Refrigerate, on tray, for 30 minutes, or until glaze is set.

13. Scrape glaze from tray; reheat, and set in saucepan in ice water again to chill. Spoon glaze over chicken breasts, coating completely.

14. Press both kinds of olive into glaze to decorate. Refrigerate until glaze is set – about 1 hour.

15. To serve: Arrange chicken breasts in a single layer in a large, shallow serving dish. Garnish with watercress sprigs.

MAKES 8 SERVINGS

CHICKEN BREASTS FLORENTINE

3 (12-oz size) whole chicken breasts, split	1½ cups milk
All-purpose flour	½ cup light cream
Butter or margarine	1 egg yolk
¾ cup chicken broth	½ cup grated Parmesan cheese
2 tablespoons finely chopped onion	2 pkg (10-oz size) frozen chopped spinach
½ teaspoon salt	2 tablespoons grated Swiss or Parmesan cheese
⅛ teaspoon pepper	
Dash ground nutmeg	

1. Wipe chicken breasts with damp paper towels. With sharp knife, carefully remove skin and bone, keeping breasts intact. (Or purchase chicken breasts already boned and skinned.) Lightly coat chicken breasts on both sides with flour.

2. In ¼ cup hot butter in medium-size skillet, over medium heat, sauté chicken breasts about 10 minutes on each side. Add chicken broth; simmer, covered, 10 minutes, or until tender.

3. In ¼ cup hot butter in heavy, medium-size saucepan, sauté onion, stirring, until golden – about 5 minutes. Remove from heat.

4. Add ¼ cup unsifted flour, the salt, pepper and nutmeg; stir until smooth. Add milk, then cream, a little at a time, stirring after each addition. Return to heat.

5. Over medium heat, bring to boiling, stirring constantly; reduce heat and simmer 3 minutes, stirring. In small bowl, beat egg yolk with fork; stir in about ¾ cup hot sauce; mix well. Return egg-yolk mixture, along with ½ cup grated Parmesan, to rest of sauce in saucepan, stirring constantly. Cook, stirring, over low heat just until thickened and cheese is melted; do not boil. To keep sauce hot, cover saucepan and place over hot water.

6. Cook spinach as package directs. Turn into a sieve; drain well. Return to saucepan; mix with 1 cup cheese sauce; cover and keep hot.

7. Layer spinach in bottom of buttered 2-quart shallow baking dish. Arrange chicken breasts in single layer on spinach. Cover with rest of sauce; sprinkle with grated Swiss cheese.

8. Broil, 6 inches from heat, 4 to 5 minutes, or until lightly browned.

MAKES 6 SERVINGS

BRAISED CHICKEN SUPREME

3 whole chicken breasts, split (about 3 lb in all)	3 tablespoons all-purpose flour
1 can (6 oz) whole mushrooms	1 cup dry white wine
¼ cup butter or margarine	1½ teaspoons salt
½ cup coarsely chopped onion	½ teaspoon pepper
	½ cup light cream
	Watercress sprigs

1. Wipe chicken with damp paper towels.

2. Drain mushrooms, reserving ¼ cup liquid.

3. In hot butter in large skillet with tight-fitting cover, or a Dutch oven, sauté chicken, a few pieces at a time. Remove chicken as it browns.

4. In same skillet, over medium heat, sauté onion and mushrooms about 5 minutes, stirring to loosen browned bits in pan.

5. Remove from heat; stir in flour combined with reserved mushroom liquid. Stir in white wine. Add chicken, salt and pepper.

6. Bring just to boiling; reduce heat, and simmer, covered, 45 minutes, or until chicken is tender.

7. Slowly stir in cream; heat gently. Serve garnished with watercress.

MAKES 6 SERVINGS

TURKEY

*W*hen it's time to think of Thanksgiving dinner and what you will serve – though you know perfectly well, and so do we – you'll be grateful for the section on the frozen turkey that follows. (Actually, in these days of the frozen turkey, any time of year is turkey time!) Your planning will start with a plump, full-breasted bird, done to a crisp-skinned gold. Our step-by-step way will show you how.

One of the many things to be thankful for is that turkey is so nutritious, so available, so economical, so tasty, so popular with just about everybody. Today's better-bred turkey is a rich source of protein and one of the lowest in calories. Very few meats can equal its great versatility – it's good so many ways. Turkey is one leftover no one seems to mind, and everyone seems to count on. It has endless possibilities, endless treats. And after you've enjoyed the meat in every possible form, there's always the most heavenly soup to be made from the bones!

TIMETABLE FOR ROASTING

(Turkey and dressing should be at room temperature)

Ready-to-cook weight	Oven Temperature	Approximate roasting time
8 to 12 lb	325F	4 to 4½ hours
12 to 16 lb*	325F	4½ to 5½ hours
16 to 20 lb**	300F	5½ to 7 hours

Note: For unstuffed turkeys, reduce roasting time approximately 5 minutes per pound.

*Roast breast side down 2½ to 3 hours; then breast side up rest of time.

**Brush turkey breast with liquid gravy seasoning as directed on label. Roast breast side down throughout roasting time.

HOW TO CARVE ROAST TURKEY

1. Turkey is placed with legs to carver's right. Plunge fork into bird just below breast, to give firm support, being careful not to puncture breast. With carving knife, slice thigh and leg from body *(diagram a)*.

2. Pull thigh and leg away – joint should give easily *(diagram b)*. If necessary, cut through joint at socket, using a sharp, small auxiliary knife. Lift to small platter, to carve later.
3. Grasp wing in left hand; pull from body as far as possible. Work knife through joint; twist wing from body *(diagram c)*. Place on small platter.
4. Carve thin slices (parallel to breastbone) the full sweep of the breast, from top to bottom *(diagram d)*. Slice enough breast meat for first servings.
5. Holding leg in left hand, separate it from thigh, with small knife *(diagram e)*.
6. Holding thigh with fork, cut long, thin slices, with auxiliary knife. Then, holding leg in hand, carve thick slices *(diagram f)*. Include white and dark meat in each serving. Carve other side of turkey for second servings.

ROAST TURKEY À L'ORANGE
(pictured on pages 46-47)

14-to-16-lb ready-to-cook turkey	1 medium onion, peeled and quartered
Pecan Stuffing, page 45	1 medium carrot, pared and cut up
½ cup butter or margarine, melted	½ teaspoon salt
Salt	4 black peppercorns
Pepper	1 bay leaf
1 cup Beaujolais	½ cup orange marmalade
2½ cups water	**Orange Giblet Sauce,**
1 celery stalk, cut up	**page 45**

1. Remove giblets and neck from turkey; wash and set aside for broth. Wash turkey thoroughly inside and out. Pat dry with paper towels. Remove and discard any excess fat.
2. Prepare Pecan Stuffing. Preheat oven to 325F.
3. Spoon some of stuffing into neck cavity of turkey. Bring skin of neck over back; fasten with poultry pin.
4. Spoon remaining stuffing into body cavity; do not pack. Insert four or five poultry pins at regular intervals. Lace cavity closed with twine, bootlace fashion; tie.
5. Bend wing tips under body, or fasten to body with poultry pins. Tie ends of legs together. Insert thermometer in inside of thigh at thickest part.

6. Place turkey in shallow roasting pan. Brush with some of butter; sprinkle with salt and pepper. Add wine.

7. Roast, uncovered and brushing occasionally with remaining butter and pan drippings, about 4½ hours, or until meat thermometer registers 185F. Leg joint should move freely. When turkey begins to turn golden, cover with a loose tent of foil, to prevent overbrowning.

8. Meanwhile, place giblets (reserve liver) and neck in a 2-quart saucepan. Add 2½ cups water, then celery, onion, carrot, ½ teaspoon salt, the peppercorns and bay leaf.

9. Bring to boiling; reduce heat; simmer, covered, 2½ hours, or until giblets are tender. Discard neck. Remove giblets from broth; chop coarsely. Strain cooking broth, pressing vegetables through sieve with broth. Measure broth; there should be 1½ cups. Set aside.

10. Remove foil. Spread turkey with marmalade; roast 10 minutes longer. Place turkey on heated serving platter. Remove twine and poultry pins. Let stand 20 to 30 minutes before carving. Meanwhile, make Orange-Giblet Sauce.

11. To serve: Garnish with Fresh-Cranberry Sauce in Orange Shells, below. Pass Orange-Giblet Sauce.

12. If desired, decorate turkey with Candied Orange-Ring Chain, page 48.
MAKES 16 SERVINGS

PECAN STUFFING

12 cups fresh white-bread cubes	2 teaspoons salt
1 cup coarsely chopped pecans	½ teaspoon pepper
½ cup chopped parsley	½ cup butter or margarine
1 tablespoons poultry seasoning	3 cups chopped celery
	1 cup chopped onion

1. In large bowl, combine bread cubes, pecans, parsley, poultry seasoning, salt, pepper; toss to mix well.

2. In hot butter in medium skillet, sauté celery and onion until golden – 7 to 10 minutes.

3. Add to bread mixture; toss lightly until well mixed.

4. Use to fill prepared turkey.
MAKES 12 CUPS, ENOUGH TO STUFF A 16-POUND TURKEY, 16 SERVINGS

ORANGE-GIBLET SAUCE

Fat from drippings	1 tablespoon catsup
Liver from turkey	Dash pepper
3 tablespoons brandy	1½ cups broth from giblets
3 tablespoons coarsely grated orange peel	½ cup red wine
¾ teaspoon chopped garlic	¼ cup orange juice
¼ cup all-purpose flour	1 cup orange sections

1. Strain drippings into a 4-cup measure. Skim fat from surface; reserve.

2. In 2 tablespoons reserved fat in large skillet, brown liver; remove from heat. Heat brandy slightly; ignite; pour over liver. Remove liver; chop. In same skillet, in 1 tablespoon fat, sauté orange peel and garlic 3 minutes.

3. Pour 1 cup drippings back into roasting pan. Add flour. Cook, over medium heat, stirring, until flour is browned. Add catsup, pepper, giblet broth, wine, orange juice, liver, orange-peel mixture and chopped giblets.

4. Bring to boiling, stirring to dissolve browned bits in pan. Reduce heat; simmer 10 minutes. Add orange sections; heat 1 minute.
MAKES 4 CUPS, 16 SERVINGS

FRESH-CRANBERRY SAUCE IN ORANGE SHELLS

4 cups fresh cranberries	4 medium oranges (optional)
1½ cups sugar	
1½ cups water	

1. Wash cranberries; remove any stems (if frozen, don't thaw).

2. In large saucepan, combine sugar with 1½ cups water; bring to boiling, stirring until sugar is dissolved. Cook, uncovered and stirring occasionally, 10 minutes.

3. Add cranberries; return to boiling. Reduce heat; simmer, uncovered, 8 to 10 minutes. Remove from heat.

4. Turn into a bowl; refrigerate, to chill well before serving.

5. If desired, make orange shells: With sharp knife, cut oranges in half crosswise, making a zigzag pattern. Scoop out pulp (to use another time). Fill shells with cranberry sauce.
MAKES 4 CUPS, 8 SERVINGS: DOUBLE RECIPE TO SERVE 16

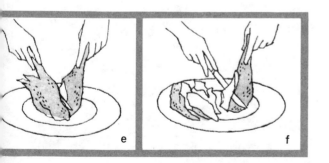

e   f

Roast Turkey à l'Orange, Fresh-
Cranberry Sauce in Orange Shells,
recipes on pages 44-45;
Candied Orange Ring Chain,
recipe on page 48.

CANDIED ORANGE-RING CHAIN
(pictured on pages 46 to 47)

5 large navel oranges
1½ cups sugar
½ cup light corn syrup

2 cups water
1 drop red food color
   (optional)

1. With 2¼-inch round cookie cutter, cut four rounds of orange peel from each orange (pressing cutter and turning into orange). With 1½-inch round cookie cutter, cut in centers of large rounds to make rings.
2. In heavy, 4-quart Dutch-oven, combine sugar, corn syrup and 2 cups water. Bring to boiling, stirring constantly until sugar is dissolved. Boil, uncovered, 10 minutes.
3. Add orange rings; reduce heat; simmer 50 to 60 minutes, or until rings are glazed. Remove from heat.
4. Turn into a shallow dish, so rings are covered with syrup. Cover; let stand at room temperature several hours.
5. To assemble chain: Make a cut in half of the rings, and interweave with remaining rings, alternating cut and uncut rings. Secure cut rings with small piece of toothpick. Stud rings with cranberries if desired.

TURKEY AU VIN

8½-to-9-lb ready-to-cook
   turkey
6 tablespoons butter or
   margarine, softened
6 slices bacon, cut in
   1-inch pieces
½ cup chopped onion·
1 clove garlic, crushed
2 tablespoons brandy
2½ cups red Burgundy
   wine
1 can (10¾ oz)
   condensed chicken
   broth, undiluted

2 teaspoons salt
½ teaspoon dried thyme
   leaves
½ teaspoon pepper
2 bay leaves
4 large sprigs parsley
Tops from 2 celery stalks
16 small white onions,
   peeled
12 medium mushrooms
16 small new potatoes
⅓ cup all-purpose flour
2 tablespoons chopped
   parsley

1. Remove giblets and neck from turkey; wash; set aside. Wash turkey inside and out. Pat dry with paper towels. Remove, discard excess fat.
2. Preheat oven to 400F.
3. Place heart, neck, and gizzard inside turkey; reserve liver. Bring skin of neck over back; fasten with poultry pin. Bend wing tips under body, or fasten to body with poultry pins. Tie ends of legs together.
4. Place turkey, breast side up, in shallow roasting pan without rack. Brush 2 tablespoons butter over turkey.
5. Roast, uncovered, 40 minutes; brush well with pan drippings; roast 10 minutes longer, or until browned. Remove from oven.
6. Meanwhile, in 8-quart Dutch oven (about 10 inches wide, 13 inches long), sauté bacon until

crisp. Remove bacon; reserve. Pour fat into a cup. Return 2 tablespoons fat to Dutch oven; add 2 tablespoons butter.
7. To butter mixture, add chopped onion and garlic; sauté until golden. Place turkey, breast side up, in Dutch oven. In large cooking spoon, warm brandy; ignite and pour over turkey.
8. When flame dies, turn turkey breast side down. Add 2 cups Burgundy, the cooking liquid with browned particles scraped from roasting pan, chicken broth, salt, thyme, pepper, bay leaves, parsley sprigs, and celery tops; bring to boiling. Reduce heat, and simmer, covered, 30 minutes.
9. In medium skillet, in 2 tablespoons hot butter, brown whole onions. Remove as browned; set aside. Add mushrooms to skillet, and sauté.
10. Turn turkey breast side up. Add onions and mushrooms to Dutch oven; simmer, covered, 45 to 50 minutes, or until turkey and vegetables are tender. Add liver; simmer 15 minutes.
11. Meanwhile, scrub potatoes; pare a narrow band of skin around center of each. In 1-inch boiling salted water in medium skillet, cook potatoes, covered, 20 to 25 minutes, or until tender. Drain. Keep warm.
12. Remove turkey and vegetables to heated serving platter. Sprinkle bacon over vegetables. Keep warm.
13. Remove and discard celery, parsley, and bay leaves. Measure liquid in Dutch oven; it should measure 4 cups. (If more, reduce by boiling.)
14. Blend flour with remaining Burgundy. Stir into pan liquid; bring to boiling, stirring boil until sauce thickens; simmer 5 minutes.
15. Spoon some sauce over turkey and vegetables; pass rest. Sprinkle chopped parsley over vegetables.

Makes 8 servings
Note: If desired, make day ahead. Cool completely before storing, covered, in refrigerator. Reheat slowly, covered, in 350F oven 1 to 1¼ hours.

TURKEY BREAST MARSALA

4 to 6 tablespoons butter
   or margarine
8 slices (¼ inch thick)
   cooked turkey breast
   (about 1¼ lb)
Dash pepper

8 thin slices prosciutto
1 pkg (8 oz) mozzarella
   cheese, cut in 8 slices
½ cup Marsala
Chopped parsley

1. Heat 4 tablespoons butter in large, attractive skillet. Sauté turkey slices, in single layer, until golden on both sides – 1 minute on each side. Add more butter as needed. Remove turkey slices as browned, and keep warm.
2. Return all slices to skillet, overlapping. Sprinkle

with pepper. Place a slice of ham and one of cheese on each slice of turkey. Pour Marsala over all.

3. Cook, covered, 3 to 5 minutes, or until heated through and cheese is melted. Sprinkle with chopped parsley. Garnish with watercress, if desired. Serve in skillet.

MAKES 4 SERVINGS

ROAST BREAST OF TURKEY

5-to-5½-lb turkey breast (see Note)
⅓ cup butter or margarine, softened
2½ teaspoons dried tarragon leaves
2½ teaspoons dried oregano leaves
2 teaspoons salt
⅛ teaspoon pepper
2 cups water
2 sprigs parsley
10 white onions, peeled
1 can (8 oz) tomatoes, undrained
2 green or red peppers, sliced
2 lb zucchini, thickly sliced
¼ cup unsifted all-purpose flour
2 tablespoons butter or margarine

1. Preheat oven to 325F.
2. Wash turkey inside and out under cold running water. Dry.
3. Combine ⅓ cup softened butter with 2 teaspoons tarragon and 2 teaspoons oregano. Put half of butter mixture in cavity of turkey breast.
4. Rub outside of turkey with rest of butter mixture. Sprinkle with 1 teaspoon salt and the pepper.
5. Place turkey in shallow, 15-by-10-inch roasting pan without rack. Insert meat thermometer into thickest part of breast. Roast, basting several times with pan drippings, 3 hours, or until meat thermometer registers 185F. Remove to heated platter. Keep warm.
6. About 30 minutes before turkey is done, cook vegetables: In 11-inch skillet with tight-fitting cover, bring 2 cups water, the remaining salt, tarragon and oregano and the parsley to boiling.
7. Add onions; cook, covered, over medium heat 20 minutes.
8. Add tomatoes. Layer peppers and zucchini over onions and tomatoes. Cook, covered, 10 minutes, or just until vegetables are tender. Drain, reserving liquid (about 2 cups).
9. In small saucepan, combine ¾ cup pan drippings (if necessary, add water to measure ¾ cup) with flour; mix well. Stir in reserved liquid. Bring to boiling, stirring. Serve as sauce.
10. Return vegetables to skillet and cook, uncovered, several minutes, to dry out vegetables. Toss with butter.
11. Serve turkey breast surrounded by vegetables.

MAKES 10 TO 12 SERVINGS

Note: If turkey is frozen, let thaw completely in refrigerator.

BREAST OF TURKEY WITH HAM STUFFING

Ham Stuffing
⅓ cup milk
2 eggs
1 tablespoon catsup
1 tablespoon prepared mustard
⅛ teaspoon pepper
⅔ cup soft white-bread crumbs
1 lb ground smoked ham
2 tablespoons finely chopped onion
1 tablespoon chopped parsley

5-to-8-lb frozen turkey breast, thawed (see Note)
2 teaspoons salt
½ teaspoon pepper
1 teaspoon dried thyme leaves
¼ cup butter or margarine, melted
2 cans (10¾-oz size) condensed chicken broth, undiluted
4 cups water
1 medium onion, quartered
3 stalks celery, cut up
1 medium carrot, cut up
1 bay leaf, crumbled
5 black peppercorns
2 parsley sprigs
2 tablespoons all-purpose flour

1. **Make Ham Stuffing.** In large bowl, combine milk, eggs, catsup, mustard and ⅛ teaspoon pepper; beat until well blended. Stir in bread crumbs; let mixture stand several minutes. Add ham, chopped onion and parsley; mix well.
2. Wash turkey breast inside and out under cold running water. Dry well with paper towels.
3. Preheat oven to 325F. With sharp knife, bone turkey, being careful not to cut skin of breast. Carefully cut around breastbone and remove; reserve bone. Lay breast flat, skin side down. Combine salt, pepper and thyme leaves. Rub half of mixture into meat.
4. Spread ham filling evenly over surface of turkey. Close breast with skewers; lace together with string. Rub rest of thyme mixture into skin of turkey. Place on rack, skewer side down, in shallow roasting pan. Brush top with melted butter. Roast, uncovered, 2 to 2½ hours, or until nicely browned. Baste with pan drippings every half hour or so.
5. Meanwhile, in large saucepan, cook turkey bones with chicken broth, 4 cups water, quartered onion, celery, carrot, bay leaf, peppercorns and parsley. Simmer, uncovered, 2 hours, or until broth is reduced to about 2 cups.
6. When turkey is done, remove to heated platter. Make gravy: Into pan drippings, stir 2 tablespoons flour; cook, stirring, until slightly brown. Pour in 2 cups turkey broth, dissolving browned bits in pan. Bring to boiling; reduce heat and simmer, stirring, until thickened – about 5 minutes. Strain.
7. Slice turkey breast with stuffing. Serve with gravy. This dish is also very nice served cold.

MAKES 12 SERVINGS

Note: If turkey is frozen, let thaw completely in refrigerator.

DELUXE TURKEY PIE

4¾ lb frozen turkey breast, thawed
1 whole onion peeled, stuck with 4 whole cloves
3 carrots, pared and thickly sliced
3 stalks celery, sliced thick
1½ tablespoons salt
10 black peppercorns
2 bay leaves
2 cans (10¾-oz size) condensed chicken broth, undiluted
Water
1 pkg (11 oz) piecrust mix
10 small white onions, peeled
4 medium carrots, pared and quartered
3 large potatoes (1¼ lb), peeled, cut into ½-inch cubes
6 slices bacon, quartered
½ lb pork sausage, formed into 12 (1-inch) balls
1 can (8 oz) sliced mushrooms
⅓ cup unsifted all-purpose flour
1 teaspoon salt
Dash pepper
2 tablespoons chopped parsley
1 egg, slightly beaten

1. Place turkey breast in large kettle (about 9-quart size), skin side down. Add whole onion, sliced carrot, celery, 1 tablespoon salt, peppercorns, bay leaves and chicken broth with water to make 7 cups.
2. Bring to boiling; reduce heat; simmer, covered, 1 hour. Turn turkey; simmer ½ hour longer, or until tender.
3. Meanwhile, prepare piecrust mix as package label directs; refrigerate
4. Remove turkey to large bowl. Strain broth, mashing vegetables, into a medium saucepan. Add white onions, quartered carrot and potato; bring to boiling; reduce heat and cook until carrots are tender – about 20 minutes.
5. At same time, in large skillet, cook bacon until crisp; drain on paper towels; pour off fat. Crumble bacon.
6. In same skillet, cook sausage balls, turning until browned all over – about 15 minutes.
7. Cut turkey meat into 1-inch cubes; it should measure 6 cups.
8. Drain broth from vegetables into a 1-quart measure. Add enough water to make 3½ cups liquid. Pour back into saucepan; bring to boiling.
9. Drain liquid from mushrooms into a 1-cup measure; add water to make 1 cup. Combine with flour in small bowl, stirring until smooth. Add slowly to boiling liquid, stirring with wire whisk until smooth and thickened. Add salt and pepper.
10. Turn vegetables into a 3-quart oval casserole or Dutch oven. Add cut-up turkey, sausage balls,

drained mushrooms, chopped parsley and thickened sauce; stir just to combine. Top with bacon. Preheat oven to 400F.
11. On lightly floured surface or pastry cloth, roll out pastry ½-inch larger all around than top of casserole. Place on top of casserole, turning edge under, press to rim of casserole, to seal all around. Cut several steam vents in top. Brush lightly with egg. Bake 30 to 35 minutes, or until crust is golden and mixture is bubbly.
MAKES 10 TO 12 SERVINGS

TURKEY EN CASSEROLE

3 lb turkey legs and thighs, cut at joints (2 whole legs and thighs or 4 drumsticks)—see Note
6 slices bacon, diced
2 tablespoons butter or margarine
8 small white onions, peeled
8 small whole mushrooms
1 clove garlic, crushed
2½ tablespoons all-purpose flour
1 teaspoon salt
⅛ teaspoon pepper
¼ teaspoon dried thyme leaves
2 cups Burgundy wine
1 can (10¾ oz) condensed chicken broth, undiluted
8 small new potatoes, scrubbed
Chopped parsley

1. Wash turkey and dry on paper towels.
2. In a 5-quart Dutch oven, over medium heat, sauté bacon until crisp. Remove and drain on paper towels.
3. Add butter to bacon drippings; heat. In hot fat, brown turkey well on all sides – 15 to 20 minutes. Remove as it browns. Preheat oven to 400F.
4. Pour off all but 2 tablespoons fat from Dutch oven. Add onions, mushrooms and garlic to Dutch oven. Over low heat, cook, covered and stirring occasionally, 10 minutes.
5. Remove from heat; stir in flour, salt, pepper and thyme. Gradually add Burgundy and chicken broth; bring mixture to boiling, stirring.
6. Remove from heat. Add potatoes, turkey and bacon to Dutch oven; mix well.
7. Bake, covered, about 2½ hours, or until turkey is tender.
8. Sprinkle with chopped parsley before serving.
MAKES 4 SERVINGS
Note: If frozen, thaw completely in refrigerator.

Roast Duckling with Olives, recipe on page 52.

DUCKLING

*T*hough, truthfully, any season is open season —
thanks to the miracle of freezing – duckling seems
particularly perfect for late-autumn dining. If you are
new to cooking duckling, this tip will help you . . .
To truss duckling: *Fasten skin of neck to back, with
poultry pin. Fold wing tips under body, to secure wings
close to it. Then close body cavity with poultry pins.
Lace (as for shoe) with twine. Tie ends of legs together.*

ROAST DUCKLING WITH OLIVES
(pictured on page 51)

6-lb ready-to cook
  duckling (see Note)
12 pitted green olives,
  coarsely chopped
1/3 cup chopped onion
Salt
Ground nutmeg
Dried thyme and
  marjoram leaves
3 lb medium potatoes
1/2 cup butter or
  margarine, melted
1/2 cup dry white
  vermouth or wine

1 tablespoon chopped
  shallot
1 tablespoon chopped
  parsley
2 tablespoons all-
  purpose flour
1 1/2 cans (10 3/4-oz size)
  condensed chicken
  broth, undiluted
1/2 teaspoon salt
Dash white pepper
1/2 cup dry white
  vermouth or wine
8 pitted green olives,
  chopped

Olive Sauce

Duck liver, chopped

8 whole green olives

1. Preheat oven to 450F. Remove giblets and neck
from duckling; set liver aside for sauce. Wash duckling well; drain and dry with paper towels.
2. Bring skin of neck over back; fasten with poultry
pin.
3. Combine 12 chopped olives, the onion, 1 teaspoon salt, dash nutmeg, and 1/2 teaspoon each
thyme and marjoram; mix well. Use to fill cavity of
duckling.
4. Close body cavity with poultry pins; lace with
twine. Tie ends of legs together; bend wing tips under body.

5. Combine 1 1/2 teaspoons salt, 1/2 teaspoon nutmeg, and 1/2 teaspoon each thyme and marjoram;
mix well; sprinkle over both sides of duckling.
6. Place, breast side down, on rack in shallow roasting pan; roast, uncovered, 30 minutes. Reduce
oven temperature to 375F. Turn duckling on other
side; roast 40 minutes longer. With baster, remove
drippings from pan as they accumulate, reserving 1/4
cup for sauce.
7. Meanwhile, pare potatoes; cut in half.
8. Again turn duckling breast side down, using 2
wooden spoons. Arrange potatoes in pan around
duckling; brush with butter. Roast 20 minutes.
9. Turn duckling, breast side up; pour 1/2 cup vermouth over it. Turn potatoes; brush with remaining
butter. Roast 30 minutes longer.
10. While duckling is roasting, **make olive sauce:**
In reserved 1/4 cup drippings in medium skillet, sauté
liver, shallot, and parsley over low heat about 5
minutes. Stir in flour; cook, stirring, a few minutes
to brown flour slightly. Remove from heat; stir in
chicken broth, salt, pepper, and vermouth. Cook
stirring, until sauce is thickened and smooth; add
chopped olives.
11. To serve: Arrange duckling on platter with potatoes and whole olives. Serve with olive sauce.
MAKES 4 SERVINGS
Note: For 6 to 8 servings, roast 2 small ducklings
(4-pound size); double recipe, but do not double
potatoes or sauce.

DUCKLING À L'ORANGE

5-lb ready-to-cook
  duckling (if frozen,
  thaw completely)
1 teaspoon salt
1 large onion, peeled
1 clove garlic, chopped
3 black peppercorns
2 unpeeled oranges,
  quartered
½ cup Burgundy
2 cups water

Orange Sauce
3 tablespoons butter or
  margarine
Liver from duckling
3 tablespoons brandy
2 tablespoons grated
  orange peel

¾ teaspoon chopped
  garlic
2 tablespoons all-
  purpose flour
2 teaspoons catsup
1 chicken-bouillon cube
Dash pepper
1¼ cups broth from
  giblets
⅓ cup Burgundy wine
¼ cup orange
  marmalade
¼ cup orange juice
1 cup orange sections

½ cup orange
  marmalade

1. Remove giblets and neck from duckling and reserve. Wash duckling under running water; drain; dry with paper towels. Turn breast side down; using sharp scissors and knife, carefully cut out wishbone from breast for easier carving. Preheat oven to 425F.
2. Sprinkle inside with ½ teaspoon salt. Tuck onion inside neck; bring skin of neck over back. Fasten with poultry pins. Stuff body cavity with garlic, black peppercorns and oranges. Close cavity with poultry pins. Tie legs together; bend wing tips under body.
3. Place on rack in shallow roasting pan. Pour ½ cup Burgundy over duckling. Roast, uncovered, 30 minutes. Reduce oven to 375F; roast 1½ hours. Bring giblets to boiling in 2 cups water and ½ teaspoon salt; reduce heat; simmer, covered, 1 hour. Strain.
4. **Make Orange Sauce.** In 2 tablespoons butter in skillet, brown liver. Remove from heat. Heat brandy slightly. Ignite; pour over liver. Remove liver; chop. In same skillet, in rest of butter, sauté orange peel and garlic 3 minutes. Stir in flour, catsup, bouillon cube and pepper.
5. Gradually add giblet broth, Burgundy, ¼ cup marmalade and the orange juice; mix well. Bring to boiling; reduce heat; simmer, stirring, 15 minutes. Add liver and orange sections; heat. Spread duckling with ½ cup marmalade; roast 10 minutes longer.
6. Remove pins and twine. Place on heated platter. Using sharp knife, cut each side of breast into diagonal slices, ½ inch wide, starting at leg. Then run knife down center of breast to separate two sides; run knife around outer edge to cut skin. Pass sauce.
MAKES 4 SERVINGS
Note: If desired, roast 2 ducklings at same time, leaving sauce recipe as is. Nice served with white rice combined with sautéed mushrooms.

Duckling à l'Orange

GOOSE

ROAST STUFFED GOOSE

Sausage Stuffing
1 lb sausage meat
2 cups finely chopped onion
1 pkg (8-oz) herb-seasoned stuffing mix
1 teaspoon salt
1/4 teaspoon pepper
1 cup water

10-lb ready-to-cook goose
1 tablespoon lemon juice
1 teaspoon salt
1/8 teaspoon pepper
White-Wine Sauce, below
Glazed Apples, below

1. **Make Stuffing.** In large skillet, cook sausage about 5 minutes, breaking up with fork into 1-inch chunks. As sausage is cooked, remove it to a large bowl. Pour fat from skillet, reserving 2 tablespoons.
2. In the 2 tablespoons hot fat, sauté onion until tender – 5 minutes.
3. Add to sausage with stuffing, salt, pepper and water, tossing lightly to mix well.
4. Preheat oven to 325F. Remove giblets and neck from goose; reserve for White-Wine Sauce. Wash goose inside and out; dry well with paper towels. Remove all fat from inside, and discard. Rub cavity with lemon juice, salt, and pepper.
5. Spoon stuffing lightly into neck cavity; bring skin of neck over back, and fasten with poultry pins. Spoon stuffing lightly into body cavity; close with poultry pins, and lace with twine. Bend wing tips under body; tie ends of legs together.
6. Prick skin only (not meat) over thighs, back, and breast very well. Place, breast side up, on rack in large roasting pan.
7. Roast, uncovered, 2 hours. Remove goose from oven.
8. Pour fat from pan, and discard. Roast goose, uncovered, 1 hour longer. Remove goose to platter; keep warm. Make White-Wine Sauce.
9. To serve, garnish with Glazed Apples. Pass White-Wine Sauce.
MAKES 8 TO 10 SERVINGS

WHITE-WINE SAUCE

Goose giblets and neck
2 1/2 cups water
1 celery stalk, cut up
1 medium onion, peeled and quartered
1 medium carrot, pared and cut up

1 teaspoon salt
4 black peppercorns
1 bay leaf
Dry white wine
2 tablespoons all-purpose flour

1. While goose is roasting, wash giblets and neck well. Refrigerate liver until ready to use. Place rest of giblets and neck in 2-quart saucepan; add 2 1/2 cups water, the celery, onion, carrot, salt, peppercorns, and bay leaf.
2. Bring to boiling. Reduce heat; simmer, covered, 2 1/2 hours, or until giblets are tender; add liver; simmer 15 minutes. Discard neck. Chop giblets coarsely; set aside.
3. Strain cooking broth, pressing vegetables through sieve with broth. Measure broth; add enough dry white wine to make 3 cups; set aside.
4. Remove goose to platter; pour drippings into 1-cup measure. Skim fat from surface, and discard. Return 2 tablespoons drippings to roasting pan.
5. Stir in flour until smooth. Over very low heat, stir to brown flour slightly. Remove from heat; gradually stir in broth.
6. Bring to boiling, stirring. Reduce heat; simmer, stirring, 5 minutes, or till thick and smooth. Add chopped giblets, salt to taste; simmer 5 minutes.
MAKES ABOUT 3 CUPS

GLAZED APPLES

1/4 cup butter or margarine
1/4 cup lemon juice
1/2 cup sugar

1/4 teaspoon salt
1/2 cup water
2 large red apples

1. In large skillet, melt butter; stir in lemon juice, sugar, salt, and 1/2 cup water. Bring to boiling, stirring, until sugar is dissolved. Reduce heat; simmer, uncovered, 5 minutes.
2. Wash apples; cut crosswise into 1/2-inch-thick slices, leaving skin on; remove cores. Place in simmering syrup, turning to coat both sides.
3. Cook apple slices, uncovered, 1 to 2 minutes on each side, or just until tender. Remove from syrup. Use as garnish around goose.

ROCK CORNISH GAME HENS

*T*hese tiny, plump-breasted, all-light-meat birds were originated in 1950 at Idle Wild Farm in Pomfret Center, Connecticut, by Therese and Jaques Makowsky. Rock Cornish game hens, a crossbreed of pure Cornish game hens descended from East Indian jungle birds and our familiar Plymouth Rock hens, are not a self-perpetuating cross. The breeding must be carefully controlled each year.

Available frozen, stuffed or unstuffed, completely boned or partially boned, Rock Cornish game hens weigh 12 to 20 ounces (ready-to-cook weight).

ROAST CORNISH HENS WITH WALNUT STUFFING AND WINE SAUCE

Stuffing
3 tablespoons bacon drippings
1 cup chopped onion
1 cup chopped green pepper
6 cooked bacon slices, crumbled
3 cups small dry white-bread cubes
1 cup coarsely chopped walnuts

1½ teaspoons salt
½ teaspoon dried thyme leaves
½ teaspoon rubbed sage

6 (1-lb size) frozen Rock Cornish hens, thawed
Basting Sauce, below
Wine Sauce, below
Watercress sprigs

1. **Make Stuffing.** In hot bacon drippings in a medium skillet, sauté chopped onion and green pepper, stirring, until tender.
2. Add vegetables to rest of stuffing ingredients; toss lightly with fork, to mix. Use mixture to stuff hens. Close openings in hens with wooden picks; tie legs together.
3. Arrange hens, breast side up, in a shallow roasting pan without a rack.
4. Preheat oven to 400F. Make Basting Sauce. Brush some over the hens.
5. Roast hens 1 hour, brushing occasionally with rest of sauce, until golden.
6. Discard string, wooden picks. Arrange hens on round platter; keep warm. Make Wine Sauce. Garnish hens with watercress.
MAKES 6 SERVINGS

BASTING SAUCE
½ cup butter or margarine
½ cup white wine

1 clove garlic, crushed
1½ teaspoons salt
½ teaspoon rubbed sage

1. Melt the ½ cup butter in small skillet. Then remove the skillet from heat.
2. Add rest of ingredients to butter in skillet, mixing well.

WINE SAUCE
3 tablespoons all-purpose flour
1 cup white wine

1 cup currant jelly
1 teaspoon dry mustard
1 teaspoon salt

1. Pour off drippings in roasting pan; return ⅔ cup drippings to pan. Gradually add the 3 tablespoons flour to the drippings, and stir to make the mixture smooth.
2. Add white wine, currant jelly, dry mustard, and salt. Bring mixture to boiling, stirring to loosen any brown bits in the roasting pan.
3. Reduce heat, and simmer the sauce, stirring occasionally, until it thickens. Pass wine sauce along with hens.
MAKES ABOUT 2⅓ CUPS SAUCE; 6 GENEROUS SERVINGS

ROAST CORNISH HENS
(pictured on page 56)
6 Cornish hens (see Note), about 1¼ lb each
¾ cup butter or margarine
¾ cup dry white wine
7 tablespoons dried tarragon leaves

Salt
Pepper
6 cloves garlic, peeled
Garlic salt
2 tablespoons all-purpose flour
1 cup water
Turkish Pilaf, page 57

1. Wash hens under cold running water; drain.
2. Make Basting Sauce. Melt butter in saucepan; stir in wine and 1 tablespoon tarragon.
3. Sprinkle inside of each hen with ¼ teaspoon salt, ⅛ teaspoon pepper and 1 tablespoon tarragon. Place one clove of garlic inside each. Sprinkle outside of each liberally with garlic salt. Refrigerate.
4. About 1 hour before serving, preheat oven to 450F. Place hens in a shallow roasting pan without a rack. Roast, basting often with sauce, 1 hour, or until hens are browned and tender.
5. Place hens on platter; keep warm.
6. Gravy: Dissolve flour in 1 cup water; stir into drippings in pan. Bring to boiling, stirring until thickened.
7. To serve: Turn Turkish Pilaf into center of platter; arrange hens on top.
MAKES 6 SERVINGS
Note: If frozen, let thaw overnight in refrigerator.

TURKISH PILAF
(pictured on page 56)

2 cups cracked wheat
2 cans (13¾-oz size)
  chicken broth
¼ teaspoon pepper

¼ cup butter or
  margarine
1 can (3 oz) chow-mein
  noodles, crumbled

1. In medium saucepan, combine cracked wheat and chicken broth. Cover; bring to boiling; reduce heat and simmer 20 minutes. Remove from heat; let stand 10 minutes longer, or until all liquid is absorbed.
2. Add pepper, butter and chow-mein noodles; toss gently to combine.
MAKES 6 TO 8 SERVINGS

ROAST CORNISH HENS AU VIN BLANC

4 Cornish hens, about
  1¼ lb each

Basting Sauce
½ cup butter or
  margarine
½ cup dry white wine
2 teaspoons dried
  tarragon leaves

Salt
Pepper
4 tablespoons dried
  tarragon leaves

4 cloves garlic, peeled
Garlic salt
1 can (10¾ oz)
  condensed chicken
  broth, undiluted
1 celery stalk, cut up
1 medium onion, peeled
  and quartered
3 black peppercorns
2 tablespoons all-
  purpose flour
¼ cup water

1. If Cornish hens are frozen, let thaw overnight in refrigerator. Wash hens inside and out under cold water; drain. Dry with paper towels. Wash giblets.
2. **Make Basting Sauce.** Melt ½ cup butter in saucepan; stir in wine and 2 teaspoons tarragon.
3. Preheat oven to 450F. Sprinkle inside of each hen with ¼ teaspoon salt, ⅛ teaspoon pepper, 1 tablespoon tarragon. Place one clove garlic, halved, inside each. Sprinkle outside of hens liberally with garlic salt, tie legs together.
4. Place close together in shallow roasting pan without rack. Roast, basting often with sauce, 1 hour, or until browned and tender. Meanwhile, place giblets (reserve liver) in medium saucepan. Add chicken broth, celery, onion, ½ teaspoon salt and the peppercorns. Bring to boiling; reduce heat; simmer, covered, 45 minutes, or until tender. Add liver; simmer 10 minutes.
5. Remove hens to heated serving platter. Pour off excess butter. Strain giblets and liver; chop; reserve broth. Combine flour and ¼ cup water; mix until smooth. Stir into drippings in roasting pan with 1 cup reserved broth and chopped giblets. Bring to boiling, stirring until thickened; add more broth, if sauce seems thick. Turn into heated gravy boat. Garnish with watercress.
MAKES 4 SERVINGS

SAUCES AND ACCOMPANIMENTS FOR POULTRY

CHICKEN GRAVY

3 tablespoons roast
  chicken drippings
3 tablespoons all-
  purpose flour
1½ cups canned clear
  chicken broth
½ teaspoon salt
⅛ teaspoon pepper

1 teaspoon coarsely
  snipped fresh
  marjoram leaves, or ½
  teaspoon dried
  marjoram leaves
  (optional)

1. Pour off drippings from roasting pan. Return 3 tablespoons drippings to pan.
2. Add flour; stir to make a smooth paste.
3. Gradually stir in chicken broth. Add rest of ingredients.
4. Bring to boiling, stirring. Simmer, stirring, 1 minute longer.
MAKES 1½ CUPS

ALMOND SAUCE FOR POULTRY

1 tablespoon butter or
  margarine
¼ cup blanched
  almonds, finely
  chopped
2 tablespoons all-
  purpose flour
1 cup chicken stock; or 2
  chicken-bouillon
  cubes, dissolved in 1
  cup boiling water

¼ teaspoon salt
Dash pepper
Dash ground mace
¼ teaspoon grated
  lemon peel
½ teaspoon lemon juice
2 tablespoons heavy
  cream

1. In hot butter in small skillet, sauté nuts, stirring frequently until golden.
2. Remove from heat. Add flour, stirring to make a smooth mixture. Gradually add chicken stock.
3. Over medium heat, bring to boiling, stirring constantly. Reduce heat; simmer 3 minutes.
4. Remove from heat. Add remaining ingredients; bring back to boiling. Delicious with roast chicken, turkey, and duck.
MAKES 1½ CUPS

TURKEY GIBLET GRAVY

Turkey giblets and neck, washed
1 celery stalk, cut up
1 medium onion, peeled and quartered
1 medium carrot, pared and cut up
1 teaspoon salt
4 black peppercorns
1 bay leaf
1 can (10¾ oz) condensed chicken broth, undiluted
⅓ cup all-purpose flour

1. Refrigerate liver until ready to use.
2. Place rest of giblets and neck in a 2-quart saucepan. Add 3 cups water, the celery, onion, carrot, salt, peppercorns, and bay leaf.
3. Bring to boiling; reduce heat; simmer, covered, 2½ hours, or until giblets are tender. Add liver; simmer 15 minutes longer. Discard neck. Remove giblets from broth, and chop coarsely. Set aside.
4. Strain cooking broth, pressing vegetables through sieve with broth. Measure broth; add enough undiluted canned broth to make 2½ cups. Set aside.
5. When turkey has been removed from roasting pan, pour drippings into a 1-cup measure. Skim fat from surface, and discard. Return ⅓ cup drippings to roasting pan.
6. Stir in flour until smooth. Stir, over very low heat, to brown flour slightly. Remove from heat. Gradually stir in broth.
7. Bring to boiling, stirring; reduce heat; simmer, stirring 5 minutes, or until gravy is thickened and smooth. Add giblets; simmer 5 minutes.
MAKES ABOUT 3 CUPS

PLUM SAUCE FOR GOOSE

1 cup port wine
⅓ cup goose drippings
1 can (1 lb, 14 oz) purple plums, drained
⅛ teaspoon ground cinnamon
Dash ground red pepper
1 tablespoon cornstarch
2 tablespoons water

1. In medium saucepan, over low heat, simmer port, uncovered, until port is reduced to about ½ cup.
2. Add drippings; cook 5 minutes.
3. Remove pits from plums; discard pits. Crush plums slightly with fork. Add to port mixture along with cinnamon and pepper; simmer 5 minutes.
4. In small bowl, combine cornstarch with 2 tablespoons water; stir to make a smooth paste. Add to plum mixture.
5. Bring to boiling, stirring; reduce heat, and simmer, stirring occasionally, until sauce is thickened and translucent – about 20 minutes.
MAKES 3 CUPS

ORANGE-CRANBERRY MOLD

4 cups (1 lb) fresh cranberries
1 cup sugar
2 navel oranges
1 env unflavored gelatine
½ cup orange juice

1. Wash cranberries; drain; remove stems; chop coarsely. Add sugar; let mixture stand 15 minutes, stirring occasionally.
2. Meanwhile, peel oranges; cut into ½-inch slices. Cut each slice into 6 pieces.
3. Sprinkle gelatine over orange juice in small saucepan, to soften – 5 minutes. Place over low heat, stirring until gelatine is dissolved.
4. Add gelatine mixture and orange pieces to cranberries; mix well. Turn into 1-quart mold.
5. Refrigerate until firm – 6 to 8 hours or overnight.
6. To unmold: Run a small spatula around edge of mold. Invert on a serving plate; place a hot, damp dishcloth on bottom of mold; shake to release. Repeat if necessary.
MAKES 8 TO 10 SERVINGS

FRESH-CRANBERRY RELISH

2 large navel oranges
4 cups (1 lb) fresh cranberries
2 unpared red apples, cored
2 cups sugar

1. Peel oranges; reserve half of 1 peel. Chop oranges coarsely.
2. Wash cranberries; drain, and remove stems. Put cranberries, apples, and reserved orange peel through coarse blade of food chopper. Add oranges and sugar; mix well.
3. Refrigerate several hours, or overnight.
MAKES 1 QUART

SPICED CRANBERRIES

4 cups (1 lb) fresh cranberries
1½ cups water
5 whole cloves
5 whole allspice
2 (3-inch) cinnamon sticks
3 cups sugar

1. Wash cranberries; drain; remove stems.
2. Turn into 3½-quart saucepan. Add 1½ cups water.
3. Tie spices in a small cheesecloth bag; add to cranberries.
4. Cook, covered and over medium heat, just until cranberries burst – about 10 minutes.
5. Remove from heat; discard cheesecloth bag. Stir in sugar; cook, stirring, over low heat, 5 minutes.
6. Cool; refrigerate covered. Serve cold.
MAKES 1 QUART

CRANBERRY-APPLE SAUCE

1 cup cranberries, washed
¾ cup sugar
2 tablespoons maple or maple-flavored syrup
¼ cup water
2 medium apples, pared, cored and chopped
2 tablespoons butter or margarine

1. In medium saucepan, combine cranberries and sugar; mash cranberries slightly with fork.
2. Add maple syrup and ¼ cup water; mix well. Bring to boiling, stirring constantly, about 3 minutes, or until cranberries pop.
3. Add apple and butter; simmer, covered, 5 minutes.

FRESH-CRANBERRY-AND CITRUS SHERBET

4 cups cranberries
Water
1 envelope unflavored gelatine
2 cups sugar
¼ cup lemon juice
1 tablespoon grated orange peel
¼ teaspoon salt

1. Set refrigerator control at coldest setting.
2. Wash cranberries; drain; remove stems.
3. In medium saucepan, combine cranberries with 2 cups water; bring to boiling, covered. Reduce heat; cook just until skins pop.
4. Meanwhile, sprinkle gelatine over ¼ cup water in small bowl; let stand 5 minutes, to soften.
5. Press cranberries and liquid through sieve, to make a purée. Stir in softened gelatine and the sugar, stirring until dissolved.
6. Stir in rest of ingredients. Pour into 2 ice-cube trays. Freeze until mushy – about 2 hours.
7. Turn mixture into large bowl of electric mixer. Beat, at high speed, until light-colored and fluffy – about 3 minutes.
8. Turn back into ice-cube trays; freeze until firm – about 2½ hours.
MAKES 2 QUARTS

FRESH-CRANBERRY SAUCE

4 cups (1 lb) fresh cranberries
3 cups sugar
2 cups boiling water
1 tablespoon grated orange peel

1. Wash cranberries; drain, and remove stems.
2. Combine with remaining ingredients in 3½-quart saucepan; let stand 5 minues.
3. Simmer, covered, 5 minutes. Remove from heat. Let stand 5 minutes.
4. Simmer, covered, 5 minutes longer. Remove from heat.
5. Cool; then refrigerate until well chilled – several hours, or overnight.
MAKES 1 QUART

POULTRY STUFFING

*E*xactly as important as the bird is the stuffing (maybe you call it dressing), and we have provided a great variety that will add a special and scrumptious elegance.

MASHED-POTATO STUFFING

10 medium potatoes (3 lb)
Boiling water
1 tablespoon salt
½ cup butter or margarine
1 cup chopped onion
½ cup chopped celery
4 cups toasted bread crumbs (see Note)
2 teaspoons salt
1 teaspoon dried sage leaves
1 teaspoon dried thyme leaves
3 eggs, beaten

1. Pare potatoes; quarter. In 2 inches boiling water in large saucepan, cook potatoes with 1 tablespoon salt, covered, until tender – 20 minutes. Drain well; return to saucepan.
2. Beat with portable electric mixer (or mash with potato masher) until smooth. Heat slowly over low heat, stirring, to dry out – about 5 minutes.
3. In hot butter in medium skillet, sauté onion and celery 5 minutes, or until tender.
4. Add mashed potato to onion-celery mixture, along with bread crumbs, salt, sage and thyme. Beat with wooden spoon to mix well. Beat in eggs. Use potato mixture to stuff turkey.
MAKES 10 CUPS STUFFING, ENOUGH FOR A 12-POUND TURKEY
Note: Toast white bread; grate on fine grater.

SAUSAGE STUFFING

1 lb sausage meat
1 cup chopped onion
2 cups chopped celery
1 cup chopped green pepper
10 cups fresh white-bread cubes
2 teaspoons salt
1 teaspoon dried tarragon leaves
1 egg, slightly beaten

1. Cook sausage meat in large skillet, stirring, until lightly browned. Remove with slotted spoon; drain, reserving 2 tablespoons drippings.
2. In reserved drippings, sauté onion, celery, and green pepper until tender – about 5 minutes.
3. In large bowl, with fork, toss lightly with remaining ingredients and sausage until well combined.
MAKES ABOUT 12 CUPS, ENOUGH TO FILL A 10-TO 12-POUND READY-TO-COOK TURKEY

SAUSAGE-CORNBREAD DRESSING

1 pkg (10 or 12 oz) cornbread mix
1 lb sausage meat
4 cups chopped celery
3 cups chopped onion
1 cup chopped green pepper
1/4 cup chopped parsley
1 1/2 teaspoon rubbed savory
1 1/2 teaspoons dried sage leaves
1 1/2 teaspoons dried thyme leaves
1 tablespoon salt
1/2 teaspoon pepper
1 can (13 3/4 oz) chicken broth, undiluted
3 eggs, slightly beaten

1. Prepare cornbread mix as package label directs. Cool.
2. In large skillet, sauté sausage meat, stirring, until lightly browned. Add celery, onion, green pepper and parsley; sauté 8 to 10 minutes.
3. Crumble cooled cornbread into large bowl. Add sausage meat, vegetables, savory, sage, thyme, salt and pepper. Gradually add chicken broth and eggs, tossing lightly with fork.
MAKES ABOUT 10 CUPS, ENOUGH FOR A 12-POUND TURKEY

CHESTNUT STUFFING

1 cup butter or margarine
1 cup chopped onion
4 cups coarsely chopped celery
1/4 cup chopped parsley
6 cups dry white-bread cubes
4-cans (about 4 lb) water-packed chestnuts (see Note), well-drained and broken into pieces
2 teaspoon salt
1/4 teaspoon pepper
1/8 teaspoon ground nutmeg
1/4 cup light cream
1/4 cup white wine

1. In hot butter in large skillet, sauté onion, celery and parsley, stirring, about 5 minutes.
2. In large kettle, combine bread cubes, chestnuts, salt, pepper and nutmeg; toss to mix well.
3. Combine cream and wine; mix well. Add to bread mixture, along with vegetables and drippings in skillet. Toss lightly, using two large forks.
MAKES 13 CUPS, ENOUGH TO FILL A 16-POUND TURKEY
Note: Or use fresh chestnuts: To roast, make a slit in each shell with a sharp knife. Bake at 500F for 15 minutes. Remove shells and skins.

JOANNE'S MARYLAND OYSTER STUFFING

1/2 cup butter or margarine
1 cup chopped onion
1 cup chopped celery
1/4 teaspoon dried thyme leaves
1/4 teaspoon salt
Dash pepper
1 1/2 lb firm-type sliced white bread, cut into cubes
2 pints small oysters
1 egg

1. In hot butter in Dutch oven, sauté onion and celery, stirring until golden – about 5 minutes. Remove from heat.
2. Stir in thyme, salt and pepper. Add bread cubes; toss lightly to mix well.
3. Drain oysters, reserving liquid. Add oysters to bread mixture; toss lightly to combine.
4. In small bowl, combine 1/2 cup oyster liquid and the egg; beat with fork to blend well. Add to bread mixture; toss lightly to combine.
MAKES 10 CUPS, ENOUGH STUFFING FOR A 12-TO-14-POUND TURKEY
Note: Or you may turn stuffing into a lightly buttered 2-quart casserole. Bake at 350F, 3/4 hour, or until oysters curl.

FRESH-MUSHROOM STUFFING

1/2 cup butter or margarine
1 cup finely chopped onion
1 1/2 lb fresh mushrooms, coarsely chopped
1 pkg (8 oz) herb-stuffing mix
1/2 cup water
1/2 cup chopped parsley
2 teaspoons dried marjoram leaves
1 teaspoon poultry seasoning
1/2 teaspoon salt
1/2 teaspoon ground nutmeg
1/8 teaspoon pepper

1. In hot butter in large skillet, sauté onion and mushrooms, stirring, about 5 minutes; remove from heat.
2. In large bowl, combine stuffing mix, water, parsley, marjoram, poultry seasoning, salt, nutmeg and pepper; toss to mix well. Add sautéed onion and mushrooms and the drippings in skillet. With two forks, toss lightly.
MAKES ABOUT 8 CUPS, ENOUGH FOR A 10-POUND TURKEY

OYSTER-AND-PECAN DRESSING

1/2 lb pork-sausage meat, broken up
1/2 cup butter or margarine
1 cup chopped onion
1 cup chopped celery
2 tablespoons chopped parsley
1 teaspoon salt
1/4 teaspoon white pepper
1/2 tablespoon Worcestershire sauce
3 cups fresh oysters, drained; or 3 cans (8-oz size) oysters, drained; or 3 cans (7-oz size) frozen oysters, thawed and drained
1 cup coarsely chopped pecans
6 cups day-old bread cubes, crusts removed

1. In 6-quart Dutch oven or kettle, sauté sausage until golden – about 5 minutes. Remove sausage; add butter to sausage fat. In hot fat, sauté onion, celery and parsley until onion is golden – 5 minutes. Remove from heat.

2. Add salt, pepper, Worcestershire, oysters, cooked sausage, pecans and bread cubes to Dutch oven. Toss lightly to mix well. Use to fill turkey.
MAKES 10 CUPS, ENOUGH FOR A 12-POUND TURKEY

SAVORY STUFFING

½ lb bacon, cut up	1 teaspoon salt
1½ cups chopped onion	1 tablespoon poultry
½ cup butter, melted	seasoning
2 quarts crumbled dry	½ teaspoon pepper
white bread (see Note)	¼ cup chopped parsley

1. In large skillet, sauté bacon and onion until bacon is crisp and onion tender. Remove from heat.
2. In large bowl, combine butter, bread, salt, poultry seasoning, pepper and parsley; toss lightly to combine.
3. Add bacon, onion and drippings; toss lightly. Use to stuff a small turkey; or bake in tightly covered 2-quart casserole 1 hour at 350F.
MAKES 2 QUARTS
Note: Or use 2 packages (8-ounce size) unseasoned stuffing mix.

CRANBERRY-ORANGE DRESSING

1 cup butter or margarine	2 loaves (1-lb size)
½ cup chopped onion	raisin-bread
½ cup chopped celery	1½ teaspoons salt
1 cup chopped Brazil	½ teaspoon poultry
nuts	seasoning
2 cups fresh cranberries,	½ teaspoon dried savory
washed	leaves
½ cup sugar	⅛ teaspoon pepper
¾ cup orange juice	
1 tablespoon grated	
orange peel	

1. Preheat oven to 350F.
2. In hot butter in medium skillet, sauté onion, celery and Brazil nuts about 5 minutes.
3. Add cranberries, sugar and orange juice and peel; cook over medium heat, stirring constantly, until cranberries start to pop. Remove from heat; let stand 20 minutes.
4. Cut bread slices into ½-inch cubes, to measure 10 cups. Spread bread cubes on a cookie sheet. Place in oven 5 minutes, or until lightly toasted.
5. Turn cubes into large bowl. Add salt, poultry seasoning, savory and pepper; toss to mix.
6. Add cranberry mixture; toss lightly until well mixed.
7. Use to fill prepared turkey.
MAKES 12 CUPS, ENOUGH TO STUFF A 16-POUND TURKEY

SWEET-POTATO-PECAN STUFFING

4 cups mashed, cooked	1½ teaspoons salt
sweet potatoes or	1½ teaspoons dried
yams	thyme leaves
1 cup butter or	1½ teaspoons dried
margarine, melted	marjoram leaves
3 cups finely chopped	½ teaspoon dried sage
onion	¼ teaspoon pepper
2 cups finely chopped	8 cups toasted bread
celery	cubes
2 cups coarsely chopped	
pecans	

1. In large bowl or kettle, mash sweet potatoes with electric mixer until smooth; beat in ½ cup butter.
2. In remaining hot butter in large skilelt, sauté onion and celery, stirring, until onion is golden – about 5 minutes. Add to potato along with pecans, salt, thyme, marjoram, sage and pepper; mix well. Add bread cubes; stir until well combined. Cool before using.
MAKES 10 CUPS, ENOUGH FOR A 12-POUND TURKEY

BREAD STUFFING

2 tablespoons butter or	2 tablespoons chopped
margarine	parsley
⅓ cup chopped onion	½ teaspoon dried thyme
1 chicken liver, chopped	leaves
3 slices white bread,	½ teaspoon salt
cubed	Dash pepper
	¼ cup milk

1. In 2 tablespoons hot butter in medium skillet, sauté onion until golden. Add liver, sauté 1 minute.
2. Remove from heat; stir in bread cubes, parsley, thyme, salt, and pepper. Add milk, tossing mixture with a fork.
3. Use to fill prepared chicken.
MAKES ENOUGH TO STUFF A 4-LB ROASTING CHICKEN

STUFFING BALLS

3 tablespoons butter or	3 cups soft bread crumbs
margarine, melted	1 egg, slightly beaten
½ cup finely chopped	½ teaspoon salt
onion	Dash pepper
2 tablespoons finely	Gravy, canned or from
chopped parsley	roast chicken

1. In medium bowl, combine all ingredients except gravy; toss lightly with fork.
2. With hands, shape stuffing mixture into balls 1 inch in diameter.
3. Add to prepared gravy; cook, covered, over low heat, 5 minutes, or until stuffing balls are heated through. Serve hot along with gravy.
MAKES 8

WILD FOWL

Is there a hunter in your family? Does he triumphantly return home bearing gifts of partridge or pheasant? Flatter him by preparing his prize according to one of McCall's special recipes.

SQUAB ITALIANO

Stuffing

8 Italian sausages
²/₃ cup thinly sliced green onions
2 cloves garlic, crushed
1¹/₃ cups thinly sliced fresh mushrooms
1¹/₃ cups sliced ripe olives
³/₄ teaspoon salt
¹/₈ teaspoon pepper
3 tablespoons olive or salad oil

1 teaspoon dried basil leaves

8 (1-lb size) ready-to-cook squab
¹/₃ cup olive or salad oil
1 can (8 oz) tomato sauce
¹/₂ teaspoon dried basil leaves

Sliced ripe olives
Parsley sprigs

1. Preheat oven to 500F.
2. **Make Stuffing.** In medium skillet, sauté sausages until well browned. Remove from skillet; drain well; remove casings; crumble meat.
3. Drain all but 1 tablespoon fat from skillet. In hot fat, sauté onions and garlic until tender – about 5 minutes.
4. Add sausage, mushrooms, olives, salt, pepper, olive oil, and basil; mix well. Use mixture to stuff squab, using about ¹/₂ cup for each. Tie legs together with twine.
5. Arrange squab on rack in shallow pan; brush with olive oil. Roast 15 minutes.
6. Reduce oven temperature to 400F. Mix tomato sauce with basil. Brush squab with some of tomato mixture. Cover pan with foil.
7. Roast 40 minutes, basting every 10 minutes with pan drippings.
8. To serve: Remove twine. Brush squab with remaining tomato mixture. Garnish with olives and parsley.
MAKES 8 SERVINGS

SQUAB IN SOUR CREAM

2 (³/₄-lb size) ready-to-cook squab
¹/₄ cup unsifted all-purpose flour
2 tablespoons butter or margarine
¹/₂ cup sliced onion
¹/₂ cup tomato juice
1 teaspoon salt

¹/₂ teaspoon paprika
¹/₂ teaspoon dried basil leaves
¹/₄ teaspoon pepper
1 can (3 oz) sliced mushrooms, undrained
1 cup sour cream

1. Rinse squab well; pat dry with paper towels. Coat well with flour.
2. In hot butter in large skillet, sauté squab until nicely browned on all sides – 10 to 15 minutes.
3. Add onion; cook, stirring occasionally, until tender – about 5 minutes.
4. Combine tomato juice, salt, paprika, basil, pepper, and mushrooms. Pour over squab; bring to boiling. Reduce heat, and simmer, covered, 20 to 30 minutes, or until squab is tender.
5. Remove squab to heated platter; keep warm.
6. Gradually add sour cream to mixture in skillet, stirring constantly. Reheat gently. Pour over squab.
MAKES 2 SERVINGS

SQUAB À LA GRECQUE

Stuffing

¹/₄ cup butter or margarine
¹/₂ cup chopped green onions
6 cups fresh white-bread crumbs
1 small clove garlic, crushed
2 tablespoons finely chopped celery
1 tablespoon chopped parsley
¹/₂ cup slivered blanched almonds
1 teaspoon salt
Dash pepper

¹/₄ teaspoon dried rosemary leaves
3 tablespoons cognac

6 (1-lb size) ready-to-cook squab
¹/₄ cup butter or margarine
2 cups sliced onion
1 cup diagonally sliced carrots
1 cup diagonally sliced celery
1 cup clear chicken broth
3 cups hot cooked white rice
¹/₂ cup dry white wine

1. **Make Stuffing.** In hot butter in medium skillet, sauté onions 5 minutes. Add rest of stuffing ingredients, tossing lightly to combine.
2. Fill cavities of squab lightly with stuffing mixture; tie legs together with twine.
3. Preheat oven to 500F.
4. In hot butter in medium skillet, sauté onion, carrots, and celery 5 minutes, stirring occasionally.
5. Transfer vegetables to shallow roasting pan; add broth. Arrange squab over top.
6. Roast 15 minutes, basting frequently.
7. Reduce oven temperature to 400F. Cover pan with foil. Roast 40 minutes longer, or until legs of birds move easily.
8. Remove squab from roasting pan; drain vegetables, reserving broth. Toss drained vegetables with rice; turn onto serving platter.
9. Arrange squab over rice mixture; place in oven to keep warm.
10. Combine wine and reserved broth; bring to boiling, stirring. Pass along with squab.
MAKES 6 SERVINGS

ROTISSERIE-BROILED SQUAB

2 (3/4-lb size) ready-to-cook squab
2 tablespoons butter or margarine
1/4 cup apricot preserves
1 tablespoon lemon juice
1/2 teaspoon dry mustard
1 teaspoon paprika
1/4 teaspoon salt
1/4 teaspoon ground ginger

1. Rinse squab; pat dry with paper towels. Bend wings under birds; tie legs together. Secure on spit.
2. In small saucepan, over low heat, cook butter and preserves, stirring, until both are melted. Remove from heat.
3. Add remaining ingredients, mixing well. Brush squab with some of mixture.
4. Broil 45 minutes, brushing occasionally with remaining mixture.
MAKES 2 SERVINGS

SAVORY PHEASANT PIE

3-lb ready-to-cook pheasant, cut up
1 bay leaf
2 celery tops
1 onion, quartered
3 medium carrots, pared
5 black peppercorns
2 teaspoons salt
1 can (3 oz) sliced mushrooms
1/2 pkg (10-oz size) frozen peas, thawed
6 tablespoons butter or margarine
6 tablespoons unsifted all-purpose flour
1/4 cup dry sherry
1 cup milk
1/2 pkg (11-oz size) piecrust mix

1. Rinse pheasant well; pat dry with paper towels.
2. In large kettle, combine pheasant, bay leaf, celery tops, onion, carrots, peppercorns, and salt with 6 quarts water.
3. Bring to boiling. Reduce heat, and simmer, covered, 1 1/4 hours, or until pheasant is tender.
4. Preheat oven to 425F. With slotted utensil, remove pheasant and carrots from stock. Place pheasant in 2-quart casserole. Slice carrots; add to pheasant.
5. Strain stock, reserving 1 1/2 cups. Also, drain mushrooms, reserving liquid.
6. Add mushrooms along with peas to pheasant.
7. Slowly melt butter in medium saucepan. Remove from heat. Add flour, stirring to make a smooth paste.
8. Combine reserved stock, reserved mushroom liquid, sherry, and milk. Gradually add to flour mixture, stirring until smooth.
9. Over medium heat, bring to boiling, stirring; boil 2 minutes. Pour over mixture in casserole.
10. Prepare piecrust mix as package label directs. On lightly floured surface, roll out to a 10-inch circle, or circle large enough to fit over casserole. Adjust over top of casserole; trim edge, and flute. Make several gashes in center of crust, for steam vents.
11. Bake 15 to 20 minutes, or until crust is golden-brown.
MAKES 4 TO 6 SERVINGS

PHEASANT WITH WILD-RICE STUFFING

3-lb ready-to-cook pheasant
2 tablespoons butter or margarine
3/4 cup diced celery
1/4 cup chopped onion
2 tablespoons chopped parsley
1 teaspoon salt
1/4 teaspoon pepper
3/4 teaspoon dried rosemary leaves
1 can (3 oz) sliced mushrooms, drained
1 1/2 cups cooked wild rice
2 or 3 bacon slices

1. Rinse pheasant well; pat dry with paper towels. Preheat oven to 325F.
2. Slowly melt butter in medium skillet. Add celery, onion, and parsley; cook, stirring, over medium heat, until vegetables are tender – about 10 minutes. Remove from heat.
3. Add remaining ingredients, except bacon, tossing gently with fork to combine.
4. Spoon stuffing lightly into neck and body cavity of pheasant. Truss pheasant, following directions for trussing Roast Wild Duck, page 64.
5. Place on rack in shallow roasting pan. Place bacon slices over breast.
6. Roast 2 hours, basting occasionally with pan drippings.
7. To serve: Remove pins and twine. Spoon stuffing into a serving dish. Cut pheasant in half or in quarters; arrange on heated platter.
MAKES 2 TO 4 SERVINGS

SAUTÉED QUAIL

4 ready-to-cook quail
1/4 cup butter or margarine
1/3 cup sliced onion
1/2 teaspoon salt
1/8 teaspoon pepper
1/3 cup sherry

1. Rinse quail well; pat dry with paper towels.
2. In hot butter in large skillet, sauté quail until nicely browned – about 10 minutes.
3. Add onion; cook, stirring occasionally, until tender – about 5 minutes.
4. Add salt, pepper, and sherry, mixing well; bring to boiling. Reduce heat, and simmer, covered, 20 minutes, or until quail are tender.
MAKES 2 SERVINGS

SMOTHERED QUAIL

4 ready-to-cook quail
1/4 cup butter or margarine
1/2 cup sliced shallots
1/4 cup cider vinegar
1 tablespoon sugar
1/2 teaspoon salt

1. Rinse quail well; pat dry with paper towels.
2. In hot butter in large skillet, sauté quail until nicely browned – about 10 minutes.
3. Add shallots; cook, stirring occasionally, until tender – about 5 minutes.
4. Add vinegar, sugar, and salt, mixing well; bring to boiling. Reduce heat, and simmer, tightly covered, 20 to 30 minutes, or until quail are tender.
5. Serve quail with pan juices spooned over.
MAKES 2 SERVINGS

BRAISED PARTRIDGES

2 (3/4-lb size) ready-to-cook partridges*
1/4 cup butter or margarine
1/3 cup sliced onion
1 can (10 1/2 oz) condensed cream-of-mushroom soup, undiluted
1/3 cup sauterne

1. Rinse partridges; dry with paper towels.
2. In hot butter in heavy skillet or Dutch oven, sauté partridges until nicely browned – about 10 minutes.
3. Add onion; cook, stirring occasionally, until tender – about 5 minutes.
4. Add soup and sauterne, mixing well; bring to boiling. Reduce heat, and simmer, covered, 25 to 30 minutes, or until partridges are fork-tender. Serve with sauce.
MAKES 2 SERVINGS
*Grouse may be substituted for partridge.

BRANDIED PARTRIDGES

2 (3/4-lb size) ready-to-cook partridges
1/4 cup butter or margarine
1 tablespoon finely chopped onion
1/2 cup chicken bouillon or broth
1/2 teaspoon salt
1 cup seedless grapes
1/4 cup brandy
2 teaspoons cornstarch

1. Rinse partridges; dry with paper towels.
2. In hot butter in large skillet, sauté partridges until nicely browned – 10 minutes.
3. Add onion, bouillon, and salt; bring to boiling. Reduce heat, and simmer, covered, 25 to 30 minutes, or until partridges are almost tender.
4. Add grapes; simmer 10 minutes longer. Remove from heat.
5. In small bowl, combine brandy and cornstarch, mixing well. Add to mixture in skillet, blending well. Bring to boiling, stirring; boil 1/2 minute. Serve partridges with sauce.
MAKES 2 SERVINGS

ROAST WILD DUCK

1 1/2-lb ready-to-cook wild Mallard duck
1/2 teaspoon salt
1/8 teaspoon pepper
3 onion slices, 1/4 inch thick
1 celery stalk
1 medium carrot, pared
3 juniper berries (optional)
2 bacon slices
1/2 cup dry white wine

1. Rinse duck well; pat dry with paper towels. Sprinkle surface and body cavity with salt and pepper. Preheat oven to 450F.
2. Stuff duck cavity with onion, celery, carrot, and juniper berries.
3. Fasten skin of neck to back, with poultry pin. Fold wing tips under body, to secure wings close to it. Then close body cavity with poultry pins. Lace with twine. Tie ends of legs together.
4. Place duck on rack in shallow roasting pan. Secure bacon slices across top; baste with wine. Roast 30 minutes, basting frequently with wine. (Roast longer if a well-done duck is desired.)
5. When duck is done, remove poultry pins and twine. Cut into serving-size pieces, and arrange on platter.
MAKES 2 SERVINGS